BARRON'S
EZ-101
STUDY KEYS

Robert D. Geise
Adjunct Professor of
American History
Park College

American History To 1877

All inquiries should be addressed to:
Barron's Educational Series, Inc.
250 Wireless Boulevard
Hauppauge, New York 11788

Library of Congress Catalog Card No. 91-35200

ISBN-13: 978-0-8120-4737-0

ISBN-10: 0-8120-4737-0

Library of Congress Cataloging-in-Publication Data

Geise, Robert.
      Study keys to American history, to 1877 / Robert Geise.
           p.   cm.
      Includes index.
      ISBN 0-8120-4737-0
      1. United States—History—Study and teaching I. Title.
E175.8.G45   1992
973.071'1—dc20   91-35200
                                              CIP

PRINTED IN CHINA
456 5500   20 19 18 17 16

CONTENTS

Theme 1 EARLY EXPLORATION AND SETTLEMENT

*T*he Western Hemisphere became the meeting ground of three great cultures: the Native American ("Indian"), the European (source of voluntary immigrants), and the African (source of involuntary immigrants, or slaves). Native Americans developed widely scattered and diverse societies. The European encounter was part of a world-wide diffusion of that civilization, impelled by a variety of motives, including economic and religious. English settlements were initially concentrated on the East coast of North America.

INDIVIDUAL KEYS IN THIS THEME

1 The first Americans

2 Impulses to European exploration

3 Early explorers

4 Early English explorers and settlements

Key 1   The first Americans

OVERVIEW *Native Americans, who peopled the Western Hemisphere thousands of years before the arrival of the first Europeans, developed diverse cultures but lacked the unity necessary for effective resistance.*

Mongoloid peoples: Appear to have migrated across a Bering Strait land bridge from Siberia perhaps 30,000 years ago, gradually spreading over the hemisphere.
- A great cultural diversity developed, including over 1,000 different languages.
- Stable agriculture, town life, and commerce characterized the "high cultures" of Central America (Maya, Aztec) and the Andes (Incas).
- Population estimates for these empires vary widely.

Native American cultures north of Mexico: Ranged from the early "mound builders" of the Ohio Valley to the "pueblo" cultures (Hopis, Anasazi) of the Southwest.
- Native Americans showed remarkable respect for and adaptation to their environment. *Example:* Use of "dry farming" and irrigation in the arid Southwest.
- Division of labor was based on gender. Male activity stressed warfare and hunting; female emphasized nurturing of children, planting and gathering of crops, and preparation of food.
- Native American technology had some crucial gaps (use of iron, the wheel).
- Political disunity (the Iroquois Confederacy was a notable exception) prevailed and inter-tribal warfare was common.

Europeans: Were initially welcomed and Native Americans often assisted in their adjustment to an alien environment.
- Native Americans were soon, however, conquered, exploited, and sometimes enslaved.
- Indian-European racial mix (Mestizos) and Indian-African blending were most common in Central and South America.
- Native population was decimated by epidemics of European diseases (especially small pox and measles).
- Native economies were shaken by European trade.
- Cultural diffusion occurred in both directions. *Example:* The diet of Europe was transformed by the introduction of corn, beans, and potatoes from the New World.

Key 2   Impulses to European exploration

OVERVIEW *As Europe emerged from the feudal Middle Ages, fundamental changes stimulated interest in overseas exploration and exploitation. Adventurous navigators sought new routes to Asia around Africa and across the Atlantic.*

Effects of Crusades: The Crusades (11th–15th centuries) were attempts by European armies to reconquer areas in the Middle East and Spain that had been absorbed by expanding Islam.
- Europeans came into contact with superior Arab cultures.
- Interest in Eastern trade was excited by the fabulous 13th century tales of **Marco Polo**.
- Traditional overland routes, such as the Silk Road, were slow and expensive.
- The Mediterranean trade was dominated by Italian city-states.
- Expansion of the Ottoman Empire (Constantinople fell in 1453) affected trade, adding to the need to find alternate routes.

Europe: Fundamental economic, political, and cultural changes in Europe in the 14th, 15th, and 16th centuries stimulated exploration.
- A commercial revival led to the rise of towns and a new merchant class.
- Deposit banking and joint stock companies created new sources of capital.
- The Italian **Renaissance** stimulated the arts and technology (movable type printing, improved maps and instruments, "caravel" ships).
- With the **Reformation,** new Protestant religions divided Christianity and contributed to rivalry and competition.
- Following incessant feudal wars, monarchs gradually strengthened their control and provided resources, money, and motivation for expansion and conquest.

Exploration: Impulses for exploration included:
- A spirit of curiosity and adventure
- Prospective wealth in precious metals, in trade, and in slaves
- The missionary impulse (the cross accompanied the sword)
- National and religious rivalries in the search for prestige.

Scandinavia: The earliest known European explorers were Scandinavians or Norse (although there is speculation over earlier possible contacts from Africa and Asia).

Key 3   Early explorers

OVERVIEW When *Europeans sailed westward for Asia they encountered the Americas. Exploitation of resources enriched some Europeans but brought tragedy to Native Americans and enslavement for African Americans.*

Portugal: Located in a geographically favorable position, Portugal's pioneers sought an all-water route around Africa to Asia.
- **Prince Henry the Navigator** sent ships to the coast of Africa.
- **Bartholomew Diaz** reached the southern tip of Africa (1488). Trading posts were set up.
- **Vasco da Gama** reached India (1498).
- The first African slaves were brought to Europe by the Portugese in the 1440s.

Christopher Columbus: Unsuccessfully sought funding from the king of Portugal for a "short voyage west to Japan." Then, after Ferdinand and Isabella completed the Christian reconquest of Spain by expelling Islamic "Moors" and Jews (1492), he secured their financial aid to "convert heathen lands."
- After a perilous voyage, three caravels reached the Bahamas where, believing he was in the Indies, Columbus misnamed the natives he encountered.
- Three more trips produced disappointing material rewards.
- Many Arawak Indians of the West Indies were murdered or enslaved.
- Columbus's voyage set in motion a vast westward migration of peoples and significant cultural interchange.

America: Named for **Amerigo Vespucci,** a Florentine merchant and navigator who made several trips to the Western Hemisphere after Columbus. Explorations led to competing European territorial claims.
- A declaration by the pope (1493) dividing the "New World" between Portugal and Spain was generally ignored.
- Iberian explorers included **Pedro Cabral** who claimed Brazil for Portugal.
- Other explorers (often Italians sailing for other nations) continued to search for a Northwest Passage.

Spanish Conquistadores (conquerors): Created a large empire in New Spain.

- **Cortez** conquered the Aztecs of Mexico; **Pizarro,** the Incas of Peru.
- **Balboa** crossed Panama to the Pacific; **Magellan**'s ship sailed around the world.
- **Ponce de Leon** landed in Florida; **Menendez** established a settlement at St. Augustine (1565).
- **Coronado** and others explored the interior in search of gold.

Spanish empire: Vast territories in North and South America were administered by a Spanish hierarchy.
- Indians (and later, African slaves) were coerced to work in mines and on farms.
- Some Catholic missionaries denounced treatment of Indians.
- The flow of wealth to Spain led to inflation and eventual economic decline.

KEY FIGURES

Christopher Columbus: A Genoese captain who sailed for Spain, his miscalculation opened the New World and its native population to European exploitation.

Ferdinand Magellan: After finding a passage through South American straits he was killed in the Philippines, but one of his ships was the first to circumnavigate the earth.

Key 4 Early English explorers and settlements

OVERVIEW *With the support of strong monarchs and capital from investment companies, England began to plant settlements in North America. The first successful one was at Jamestown, Virginia (1607).*

King Henry VIII: Broke with the pope over economic, political, and social differences (including his divorce and remarriage in 1529).
- His daughter, **Queen Elizabeth I,** encouraged Sea Dogs such as Drake and Hawkins to loot Spanish treasure ships.
- The **Spanish Armada**'s attempt to invade England was turned back (1588).
- England's naval strength could then help open trans-Atlantic ventures.
- Enclosure of land to raise sheep for a profitable woolen industry led to rural unemployment, movement to cities, and pressures for overseas settlement.
- A rising merchant class invested in *joint stock companies* (corporations) for speculation at home and abroad (the Muscovy Company was founded in 1553).
- Richard Hakluyt's books encouraged English settlement.

Early English failures: Humphrey Gilbert secured a royal charter and private investment but his attempts to establish a colony on Newfoundland failed. Walter Raleigh's "Virginia" settlement on Roanoke Island (now North Carolina) vanished (the "Lost Colony").

The Jamestown settlement: Two profit-seeking Virginia Companies (London and Plymouth) were chartered by King James I in 1606. The next year three ships landed settlers at Jamestown, Virginia.
- Great difficulty was experienced adjusting to the new environment: during "the starving time" many died of disease and insufficient food.
- **Captain John Smith,** who dominated the colonial council, enforced discipline and overcame political dissension.
- Crucial assistance was offered by Chief **Powhatan** and his Algonkian Indian Confederacy.
- **John Rolfe** (who married Pocahontas, Powhatan's daughter) successfully planted a cash crop of tobacco which was marketed despite the King's expressed distaste for "the filthy weed."

- As tobacco exports boomed, more land was put under cultivation, further straining relations with Native Americans.
- Pressure on the Indians to convert to Christianity and to become farmers also led to conflict.
- Warfare ended with a treaty "recognizing" English authority.
- In 1624 Virginia's Charter was revoked and it became a royal colony.

Virginia Society and Government:
- Over 60% of settlers arrived *indentured* (obliged to work for a set period of years to pay off their passage money).
- Later, *headrights* of fifty acres enticed settlers who bought a company share and transported themselves to the colony.
- Ninety "younge, handsome and honestly educated maydes" (young women) were sent by the Company in 1619.
- The same year a Dutch slave ship deposited twenty African blacks. It is believed they were considered indentured and that legalized slavery developed somewhat later.
- Also in 1619 the first General Assembly of Virginia met in Jamestown (including a governor, councilors, and *burgesses*).

The Plymouth Colony: The Pilgrims, "Separatists" who had left the Church of England, migrated to Holland in 1609 seeking religious tolerance. To maintain their English identity they sailed for America, with the permission of the Virginia Company.
- The *Mayflower* reached Cape Cod in 1620.
- Beyond Company control, the "Saints" (Pilgrim leaders) established a compact before landing at Plymouth.
- Although not actually a constitution, the document provided a precedent for later voluntary democratic compacts.
- Poorly prepared for the harsh climate, half of the settlers died the first winter.
- The Pokanoket Indians, who were seeking allies, befriended the colonists. **Squanto** acted as advisor and interpreter.
- Governor **William Bradford** wrote a history of the colony.
- Political decisions were made by *town meetings* and, later, by elected assemblies.

KEY QUOTATION

We solemnly and mutually, in the presence of God, and one of another, covenant and combine ourselves together in a civil body politic.

The Mayflower Compact

Theme 2 COLONIAL BRITISH NORTH AMERICA

*A*lthough settlers brought British cultural traditions and institutions with them, these were soon altered to adjust to the new environment. On the North American coast three regions (in addition to the moving frontier) developed into distinctive economic and cultural sections. Three types of colonial government developed: self-governing, proprietary, and royal. Puritanism molded New England, where commerce took on growing economic importance. The Southern Colonies began to develop plantation agriculture employing slave labor. The Middle Colonies blended the economies of the other two sections and welcomed ethnic diversity. Conflicts developed, first with Native Americans and then among social and regional groups.

INDIVIDUAL KEYS IN THIS THEME

Key 5   Puritan New England

OVERVIEW   *The Puritans were English religious dissenters, many of whom migrated to Massachusetts. From there the Puritan influence spread to other New England colonies.*

Puritanism: Began as a faction within the Church of England. It sought to return Christianity to its "pure," primitive, Biblical roots.
  • Puritans criticized the Anglican Church for retaining too much of the Roman Catholic Church's ritual and hierarchy.
  • Puritans stressed the Calvinist doctrine of *election* (pre-destination) as well as the importance of both divine grace and good works (as a sign of salvation).
  • They believed religion should be applied to daily life and to the functioning of government.
  • Puritan Congregationalists challenged the Stuart concept of centralized church-state control.
  • *Separatists* broke away from the English Church (see Key 4).

The Great Migration: The flight of Puritans to the New World lasted from 1629 to 1640.
  • King Charles I granted a royal *charter* (1629) to the Puritan-controlled Massachusetts Bay Company.
  • Perhaps 50,000 left England, the majority settling in the West Indies colonies.
  • Motives combined a sense of religious mission (a new "covenant") with economic opportunity (many settlers were from the middle class).
  • Boston became the capital and hub of the New England settlement.
  • Migration increased and decreased with political events in England (Civil War, Cromwell's Puritan Commonwealth, the Stuart Restoration).

The "Bible Commonwealth": Religion permeated society.
  • While affirming loyalty to a "purified" Church of England, Congregationalists were convinced of their special mission. ("We shall be as a city upon a hill.")
  • Each congregation was self-governing (with no hierarchy).
  • The Bible and the sermon held central importance.
  • The clergy formed a powerful intellectual elite but did not claim political power.
  • The General Court (legislature) was elected by adult male church

members (*freemen*). The charter of 1691 provided for a property-holding requirement.

- Democratic roots lay in individual congregational control and in town meetings.
- Puritans emphasized the "work ethic" and material progress.
- The somber image of the Puritans is exaggerated. "Blue laws" stressed observance on the Sabbath, but moderation, rather than a ban on worldly pleasures, was the rule.

Conflicts: Religious quarrels and challenges to orthodoxy plagued the "peaceable kingdom."

- Massachusetts became the "Mother" of other New England colonies.
- "Responsibility for fellow men" resulted in lack of privacy and intolerance toward dissenters.
- Reverend **Roger Williams**, who advocated church-state separation and defended the land rights of Indians, was banished in 1636. He founded the colony of Rhode Island.
- **Anne Hutchinson** (see below) was exiled in 1638.
- **Thomas Hooker** led migrants seeking better land into the Connecticut Valley. Its General Court adopted the **Fundamental Orders of Connecticut** (a constitution) in 1639.
- In Salem, Massachusetts, in 1692 trials for witchcraft led to twenty executions and imprisonment of over 100.
- As Puritan enthusiasm declined, a council of ministers adopted the "Half-way covenant" in 1662, permitting partial membership in the congregation.

KEY FIGURES

John Winthrop (1588–1649): An English lawyer, his Puritan convictions impelled him to migrate to Massachusetts Bay, where he was repeatedly elected governor. He was the first president of the New England Confederation (1643).

Anne Hutchinson (1591–1643): At her meetings she stressed God's gift of grace and salvation through direct contact with the divine. Tried for sedition and contempt for authority (and female presumption?), she was banished and emigrated to Rhode Island.

Key 6   Middle Colonies

OVERVIEW *The colonies that developed between New England and the Chesapeake attracted a variety of religions and nationalities and soon developed thriving economies.*

Dutch New York: Henry Hudson, sailing for the Dutch East India Company, sought a Northwest Passage through the continent. In 1609 he found the river that bears his name. Soon after, Dutch fur trading posts were established on Manhattan Island and at Fort Orange (Albany).
- New Amsterdam, the capital, was built on land purchased from the Indians by **Peter Minuit**.
- The expanding Dutch absorbed Swedish settlements on the Delaware River (1650s).
- Although the company offered large feudal tracts of land to *patroons* who would bring groups of settlers, the population remained sparse.
- New Amsterdam (New York) was a "company town" which offered little religious or political toleration.
- A mixed population, including English on Long Island, was ineffectively governed.

English New York: King Charles II of England granted the area to his brother, James, the Duke of York, after three Anglo-Dutch Wars.
- The Dutch surrendered to an English fleet without a fight (1664).
- Black slaves made up one-fifth of the diverse population of New York City.
- The Dutch influence persisted for some time.

New Jersey: Established in 1664 when the Duke of York turned over the lands between the Hudson and Delaware Rivers to two noble proprietors who divided it into East and West Jersey. In 1702 they were merged as a crown colony.

Pennsylvania: Established as a refuge for Quakers by **William Penn**, who received a royal land grant as a result of his father's friendship with the Stuart monarchy.
- The Quakers, who believed in direct inspiration from God and who refused to defer to political authority, were persecuted in England.
- As proprietor of the colony, Penn offered religious toleration as he recruited settlers with promotional literature.

- Quakers were pacifists and attempted to treat the Indians fairly. Penn learned an Indian language and purchased land by treaties.
- German and Scotch-Irish settlers who arrived later did not relate as well to the Indians.
- Some German settlers retained their cultural uniqueness (the "Pennsylvania Dutch").
- Penn's proprietary government offered more political involvement by freemen than most colonies did.
- A wide variety of national and religious groups were attracted to the colony.
- The town of Philadelphia prospered commercially, rivaling Boston.
- Philadelphia rapidly developed into a political and cultural center.
- Conestoga wagons were constructed by German farmers near Lancaster.
- Pennsylvania's farms produced abundant grain.

Delaware: At first part of Penn's royal grant, after 1701 it chose its own assembly. Its separation from Pennsylvania came during the American Revolution.

KEY QUOTATION

No man, nor number of men upon earth hath power or authority to rule over men's consciences in religious matters.

Charter of West Jersey, 1677

God hates persecution.

William Penn

Key 7   Southern Colonies

OVERVIEW *Like the pioneer settlement in Virginia, other Southern Colonies featured plantation economies growing staple export crops that required a supply of field labor.*

Maryland: The second Chesapeake Bay plantation colony was founded in 1634 under a royal proprietary charter granted to **Lord Baltimore** (George Calvert).
- The profit motive was combined with the intention to provide a haven for fellow Roman Catholics.
- An **Act of Toleration** was passed in 1649 (Key 26).
- As in Virginia, tobacco raising was profitable, creating a demand for field labor, primarily indentured servants but also African-American slaves.

The Carolinas: After his restoration, King Charles II granted a charter to eight court favorites for this large land area between Virginia and Spanish Florida. To encourage immigration, religious tolerance was provided. In 1729 it split into North and South Carolina.

North Carolina: Populated by migrants from Virginia, it developed a reputation for democratic independence. The chief export crops were tobacco and timber products.

South Carolina: First populated by planters who brought slaves with them from Barbados in the West Indies. Warring Indian tribes sold some captives to whites as slaves.
- Plantations produced tropical crops such as rice and indigo.
- The prosperous port of Charleston had an aristocratic and cosmopolitan tone (French Protestant refugees had settled there).

Georgia: The last of the English mainland colonies, founded in 1732.
- A royal charter was granted to trustees who would establish a military "buffer" between the Carolinas and Spanish Florida.
- General **James Oglethorpe**, the founder, was a promoter of prison reform and sought to make the colony a refuge for debtors.
- Initially alcohol and slaves were forbidden in the colony.
- A varied population included large numbers of Germans.
- In 1753, when the charter expired, Georgia became a royal colony.

Key 8   Colonial economies

OVERVIEW *Economic systems varied widely through the British North American colonies. Sectional economic differences were largely determined by variations in climate and geography.*

Agriculture: Land acquired by European settlers had been transformed to a limited extent by Native Americans who had already occupied it.
- Throughout the colonial period over 90% of the economy was agricultural.
- Most early settlers engaged in subsistence (self-sufficient) farming; this pattern continued on the frontier.

New England: A harsh climate and rocky soil made farming difficult and led to a diversified economy.
- Land was usually granted to a group (often a congregation) and then *towns* subdivided it among families.
- Profitable fishing industry included whaling (oil was used for lighting).
- Shipbuilding and coastal and trans-Atlantic commerce were economically important.
- Some small-scale manufacturing began despite discouragement from Britain.

Middle-Atlantic economy: Blended economies of the other two regions.
- This area became the colonial "bread basket" as its climate and soil produced a grain surplus.
- River systems and ports such as Philadelphia and New York City provided access to the back country and to overseas commerce.
- Merchants and artisans flourished in coastal towns.

Southern Colonies: With a favorable climate and abundant land, developed the *plantation* system.
- Staple export crops were often grown on large estates. *Examples:* tobacco in Virginia, rice and indigo dye in South Carolina.
- 50-acre *headrights* went to settlers (see Key 4).
- Southern farms tended to be scattered; there was less urban development.

Frontier areas: Provided opportunities for venturesome individuals.
- Conditions were harsh on isolated farms.
- Beyond the reach of government authority, both individual and cooperative efforts were necessary.

Key 9   Society and labor

OVERVIEW *Although most voluntary settlers were transplanted Europeans, the economic conditions in the colonies and the evolution of the slave system produced a significantly different social structure.*

Population: Growth in British North America was extraordinary.
- Despite high infant mortality and low life expectancy (though higher than in Europe), population doubled each generation.
- Population in the thirteen mainland colonies had reached 2.5 million by 1775, and 4 million by the 1790 census.
- Men outnumbered women, particularly in the early period, resulting in somewhat better status for females than in Europe.
- African-Americans constituted nearly 20%. Indians were not counted.

Women: Tended to marry early and bear many children.
- Married women were deprived of most legal rights.
- Most women were limited to domestic roles, but some became active in farming, crafts, business, and education.

Family: The basic social and economic unit.
- Children were economic assets in an agricultural society and families tended to be large.
- Parents taught children their gender roles and responsibilities.
- Epidemic diseases, such as smallpox, diphtheria, and, in the South, malaria took heavy tolls, especially in towns.

Class: Differences existed despite leveling influences, but were not as extreme as in Europe.
- The "better sort" (upper class) included wealthy merchants, Southern land-owning gentry, and professionals.
- Class status was sometimes reflected in peoples' clothing and in seating in church.
- The largest group was farmers with small holdings.
- Lowest status fell to propertyless whites, indentured servants, and slaves.
- Opportunities for upward social mobility were generally greater than in Europe.

Towns: Had 10% of colonial population by 1775.
- Philadelphia, with about 34,000 people, passed Boston as the largest city.

- Town facilities were primitive. Fires and crime were major threats to safety.
- Punishments (flogging, hanging) for crimes were harsh (Quakers in Philadelphia introduced a reform *penitentiary* system).
- Taverns, in towns and along *post roads*, were important social centers.
- Southern *tidewater gentry* (a numerically small group) often had town houses in addition to Georgian mansions on their plantations.

European ethnic mix: Greatest in the Middle Colonies (*Example:* Germans in Pennsylvania), but African-American slaves gave the South the greatest racial diversity (African-Americans were the *majority* in South Carolina through most of the 18th century).

Labor: Scarce and expensive and new sources were constantly sought.

Indentured servitude (see Key 4): A major source of labor in the colonies in the 17th century.
- Contracts provided for labor (usually seven years) to pay passage from abroad.
- English courts often sent convicts, debtors, and political prisoners as indentures.
- At termination of service, "freedom dues" (often 50 acres, equal to a headright) were usually provided.

Slavery: Gradually supplanted indenture, particularly in Southern Colonies, by the 18th century (see Key 4).
- By 1780 slaves represented 90% of the population of the British West Indies. Only 5% of the slaves brought to the Western Hemisphere entered North America.
- The earliest slave traders were the Portuguese and Dutch and, later, the English (Royal African Company, 1662).
- Peoples from West Africa, of varying languages and cultures, were captured and transported in conditions of great cruelty. Charleston, South Carolina, was the main port of entry.
- Native Americans (Indians) were rarely successfully enslaved. They sometimes provided sanctuary for runaway slaves.
- Some white Barbados sugar planters brought their slaves to the Carolinas.
- By the 1660s perpetual and hereditary servitude (a "controlled" labor supply) had become well established.
- Racial prejudice helped to implant the system.
- Laws (*slave codes*) gradually acknowledged the "peculiar institution," particularly in the South.

Key 10   Colonial culture

OVERVIEW *Colonial culture and values, originally patterned after England's, were reflected in the press and education systems and in the person of Benjamin Franklin.*

Localized cultures: Varied geographically.
- A majority of the population was illiterate and relied primarily on oral communication.
- Communities, especially in New England, focused on their churches as well as special political or civic events, such as election days or the training of the militia.
- A less concentrated population, the growth of slavery, and an Anglican church controlled from England all restrained cultural development in the South.
- In all sections a small but influential cultural elite emerged in the 18th century.

Painting: Was provincial and lacked patronage.
- Miniature portraits were popular.
- Untrained ("primitive") artists painted "genre" (realistic, everyday) scenes.
- Many painters went to Europe to study.
- Under royal patronage **Benjamin West** painted large historical scenes ("The Death of Wolfe") in his London studio.
- Colonial *sculpture* took forms such as gravestone and ship figurehead carving.

Music: Focused on religious works.
- "The Bay Psalm Book" (1640) was the earliest Colonial hymnal.
- Pennsylvania Germans stressed choral and organ music.
- Concerts were occasionally presented by musical societies.

Theater: Despite Puritan and Quaker disapproval, grew in popularity.
- English touring groups presented Shakespeare plays.
- **Thomas Kean** organized the first acting company (in Philadelphia).

Architecture: Attempted to duplicate familiar European structure but also adapt to new environments.
- New England "salt box" houses and Southern plantation houses represent extremes of regional styles.
- Swedes introduced the log cabin.

Newspapers: Became significant public influences.

- The first newspaper, *Publick Occurrences,* (Boston, 1690) was suppressed by the British governor after four days.
- Approximately forty newspapers were being published by the 1770s.
- **John Peter Zenger** was jailed by the New York Assembly in 1735 after his newspaper had criticized that body.
- At his trial for seditious libel, Zenger's defense was based on the truth of what has been printed. He was acquitted.

Education: New England was the leader, in part because of stress on the importance of Bible reading.

- In general, education was a luxury, a sign of status, and was provided primarily to males.
- A Massachusetts law of 1647 required all towns of over 50 families to provide an elementary school.
- The first colleges (Harvard, 1638; William and Mary, 1693) focused on training clergy.
- The first book printed in the colonies was the *Bay Psalm Book* (1640).
- The influential *New England Primer* (around 1690) taught the alphabet through religion.
- Southern planter gentry secured private tutors for their sons.

Benjamin Franklin: Seen as the "symbolic American" and as a personification of the Enlightenment.

- Self-educated, he was multitalented: a printer, scientist (experiments with electricity), inventor, statesman, writer (*Poor Richard's Almanac, Autobiography*).
- Civic contributions to Philadelphia helped lead that city to national prominence (a circulating library, a fire company, an academy, the American Philosophical Society).

Key 11   Colonial turmoil

OVERVIEW *Colonial stability was periodically shaken by conflict, sometimes reflecting changes in England, more often resulting from tensions in America.*

Native Americans: Frequently clashed with colonists.
- When the **Pequot** Indians resisted white expansion in Connecticut, the English and Indian allies virtually wiped out the tribe (1637).
- **King Philip's War** (1675–76) Indian attacks on Puritan towns, inflicted heavy casualties. Failure to form tribal alliances crippled the Native American resistance in New England.

Bacon's Rebellion (1676): A major popular uprising.
- Falling tobacco prices, scarcity of land for freed indentured servants, and fears of Indian attack contributed to tensions on the Virginia frontier.
- Underrepresentation in the colony's legislature and resentment toward **William Berkeley**, the royal governor, added to the unrest.
- After clashing with the Indians, rebels under the leadership of **Nathaniel Bacon** marched on Jamestown and burned the capital.
- Bacon suddenly died and the rebellion was crushed.
- The uprising reflected the tensions between tidewater aristocrats and poorer, politically deprived, frontiersmen.
- A new royal governor was ordered to restrict colonial independence or political autonomy.

Imperial control: Continued to tighten under James II.
- The *Dominion of New England* was created to unify colonial administration (1686).
- Charters were revoked, assemblies dissolved, and Governor **Andros** of Massachusetts was given extraordinary powers.

The Glorious Revolution (1689): Replaced James II with Protestant monarchs **William** and **Mary.**
- Massachusetts colonists overthrew Andros.
- In New York (Leisler Rebellion) and Maryland, popular uprisings deposed governments temporarily.
- The Glorious Revolution reasserted parliamentary power in London, but royal control was reimposed on the American colonies.

Theme 3   THE AMERICAN
REVOLUTION

*B*ritain attempted to operate its colonial empire under the profitable system later referred to as *mercantilism.* After victory over France and Spain in four inter-colonial wars, Britain attempted not only to regulate trade but also to raise revenue through taxation of the colonies. Growing resistance from Americans led eventually to the outbreak of fighting and the proclaiming of independence. Despite divided support for the cause at home, the revolutionaries were able to combine foreign aid with British blunders and with survival tactics to secure victory. Independence was accomplished, but the Revolution's impact on American society is debatable.

Key 12   The mercantile system

OVERVIEW *The implementation of the doctrine of mercantilism, which attempted to create a powerful, prosperous, nation state through regulated economic self-sufficiency, was complicated by the self-governing traditions of the British North American colonies.*

Imperial Britain: Attempted to follow a widely practiced and highly nationalistic commercial theory later known as *mercantilism.*
* Nation states were seen as pursuing the limited wealth of the world.
* Each nation sought to become economically self-sufficient.
* Another goal was to achieve a *favorable balance of trade* (the value of exports should exceed the value of imports).
* Home industries would be protected from foreign competition.
* Colonies could benefit the mother country by providing inexpensive raw materials as well as a guaranteed market for manufactured goods.
* The system should result in a net flow of gold and silver to the mother country.
* To guarantee its effective operation, mercantilism required government regulation.
* To operate profitably and safely, large merchant and battle fleets were necessary.

Legislation: Parliament passed a series of **Trade and Navigation Acts** (1651 to 1673) designed to benefit England in its commercial competition with Holland and others.
* Colonial trade was to be carried on only in English or colonial ships.
* Certain *enumerated* goods (sugar, tobacco, naval supplies, furs) could be sold only to England by her colonies.
* Nearly all foreign goods could be imported to the colonies only if they were shipped through England and paid import taxes there.
* England paid "bounties" to encourage production of some materials in the colonies.
* Later, colonies were forbidden to make or export certain goods that competed with English products (Woolen Act, Iron Act, Hat Act). Colonial interests appeared to be subordinated to those of the mother country.

The Board of Trade: Created in 1696 to deal with colonial questions.

- On advice of the Board, the Crown could disallow actions of colonial legislatures.
- The Board, an advisory group, brought a measure of efficiency to governing the empire.
- However, there were many other overlapping authorities and management was inefficient.

Colonial development: Was affected by mercantilism.

- Large numbers of black African slaves were imported to work on plantations, particularly on the West Indies sugar crop.
- Many articles not on the "enumerated" lists could be freely transported and sold abroad.
- A colonial unfavorable balance of trade drained hard currency to pay for imports.
- Debtors sought inflation through the printing of paper money.

Efforts at mercantilism: Benefitted some in the empire (ship builders in New England) and hurt others (Virginia tobacco growers).

- Some protested the policy's effects.
- Some colonists, resistant to rigid regulation, resorted to smuggling and other profitable methods of evasion.

Key 13   Wars for world empire

OVERVIEW *Europe's dynastic wars were reflected in an international struggle for colonial empire. In North America the climax was the French and Indian War.*

Balance of power wars: Erupted between England and France four times in less than a century. Each European war had a sideshow struggle in North America.
- War of the League of Augsburg (King William's War, 1689–97) tried to block expansion by King Louis XIV of France. In North America, it involved mostly frontier raids.
- War of the Spanish Succession (Queen Anne's War, 1701–13) sought to prevent the possible union of France and Spain. Border warfare occurred again in New England and in the Carolina-Spanish Florida area.
- After a preliminary skirmish with Spain known as the War of Jenkins's Ear, England fought France and Spain in the War of the Austrian Succession (King George's War, 1744–48), at the conclusion of which the status quo was restored in North America.
- Six years later (1754) warfare resumed on the North American frontier.

French colonies: New France controlled North America's most important inland waterways, extending from the St. Lawrence River through the Great Lakes, and down the Mississippi River to New Orleans.
- In a vast area underpopulated with Europeans, fur traders and Jesuit missionaries promoted friendly relations with Native Americans.

The Albany Conference: Convened by London's Board of Trade in 1754.
- Delegates from seven colonies met with Iroquois chiefs to prepare defenses.
- A Plan of Union was proposed by Benjamin Franklin:
  1. A "Grand Council" of colonies would oversee defense, Indian relations, and trade and would have tax power.
  2. A royally appointed executive would have a veto.
  3. Colonial assemblies as well as England's government rejected the plan.

The French and Indian War (1754–1763): Began in North America. Two years later it became the international "Seven Years War."

- In a strategic and disputed area, the Ohio Company, organized by Virginians under a royal charter, speculated in land and the fur trade.
- A French chain of forts (including Duquesne) was extended into western Pennsylvania to check the English.
- Virginia sent militia under young Major **George Washington** to protest French incursions.
- Washington built a stockade but was forced to surrender it (July 4, 1754).
- General Braddock, with two English regiments and colonial militia, was ambushed and routed by French and Indians en route to Ft. Duquesne (1755).
- The English deported and dispersed French "Acadians" from Newfoundland.
- In upstate New York expeditions against French forts failed.
- American colonists failed to provide a united war effort.

British victory: With **William Pitt** in charge in London and Prussian allies producing victories in Europe, the fortunes of war changed.
- With aid from their fleet, English troops took Louisbourg and the French burned and abandoned Ft. Duquesne.
- In 1759 ("The Year of Victory") attacks on Canada began to succeed. With Iroquois allies the English took Niagara and then forts on Lake Champlain. Quebec was successfully stormed (both commanders, Wolfe and Montcalm, were killed) and in 1760 Montreal fell.
- **Pontiac**, an Ottawa Chief, forged a western confederation which fought on until 1766 (see Key 14).
- England was victorious against the French and Spanish in the West Indies, the Philippines, and in India.

The Treaty of Paris (1763): England emerged as the major colonial power in the world.
- England secured all French territory in North America (to the Mississippi) as well as Spanish Florida.
- French territory west of the Mississippi became part of New Spain.
- France retained some West Indies islands.
- England's domination of India began, with Robert Clive's victories in Bengal.

Key 14 A new imperial policy (1763)

OVERVIEW *Successful conclusion of the war with France resulted in significant changes in British policies toward the North American colonies, beginning with a new policy on western lands.*

England: George III became king of England in 1760.
- The Treaty of Paris (1763) added vast areas in India and North America to the British Empire (see Key 13).
- Domestic politics involving factions within the Whig Party (which had led the Glorious Revolution in 1688) held England's attention.
- Frequent cabinet changes helped to create an unstable colonial policy.

American colonists: Had grown accustomed to running their own affairs (period of "salutary neglect," 1714–39).
- Through royal governors the colonies dealt with the monarchy more than with Parliament.
- Colonial assemblies held the right of taxation ("power of the purse").
- Colonial contributions to the war effort had often seemed half-hearted or non-existent.

Native Americans: Losers in the French and Indian War.
- With the collapse of New France, Indians were no longer able to play off European powers against each other.
- Cherokee lands in the South were opened to the English.
- **Pontiac** formed an alliance of Northwest tribes and in 1763 attacked Detroit and other English forts and settlements.
- Pontiac's war ("conspiracy") ended by treaty in 1766.

Western frontiersmen: Resented the lack of protection against the Indians.
- In Pennsylvania *Paxton Boys* massacred peaceful Indians, then marched on Philadelphia.
- In the Carolinas, *Regulators* were finally subdued by militia (Battle of Alamance, 1770).

The Royal Proclamation of 1763: Drew a line along the Appalachian Mountains.
- Americans were forbidden to settle west of the line in Indian and former French areas.
- A new Quebec colony was created west of the mountains.
- Americans soon ignored or defied the line.

Key 15   Taxation controversy (1764–66)

OVERVIEW *Parliament's efforts to raise revenue in the colonies were met with growing resistance. The repeal of the Stamp Act gave an impression of a colonial victory.*

George Grenville: The new finance minister in 1763, he sought to raise money to help pay the cost of 10,000 British troops left in the colonies for their protection. The war had doubled the British national debt.

Revenue acts: Existing laws were more strictly enforced; new legislation was enacted.
- American smuggling to evade the 1733 **Molasses Act** tax was to be halted by rigid enforcement.
- The **Currency Act** of 1764 banned paper currency as legal tender. A shortage of hard currency as a result of an unfavorable trade balance (see Key 12) had a deflationary effect.
- The **Sugar Act**, also passed by Parliament in 1764, cut the molasses tax in half but added duties on other imports and provided for enforcement.
- The **Stamp Act** of 1765 required a tax stamp on most printed material and legal documents. This alienated important colonial leaders such as lawyers, merchants, and journalists.
- A **Quartering Act** required the colonies to provide housing and provisions for British troops.

Protests: Took a variety of forms.
- **James Otis** argued in 1761 in a Boston court against *writs of assistance* (general search warrants to enforce mercantilist laws).
- Otis protested the Stamp Act by appealing to the *natural rights* of English subjects including the right to be taxed only with their consent.
- Grenville's government offered the theory of *virtual representation*: each member of Parliament represented the interests of the entire empire.
- "No taxation without (*actual*) representation" was the American slogan.
- The Virginia House of Burgesses adopted the four most moderate of **Patrick Henry**'s Stamp Act Resolves.
- Mass meetings and demonstrations by mobs occurred throughout the colonies.
- **Sons of Liberty** chapters linked resistance leaders.

- Distribution and sale of the stamps was effectively halted.

The Stamp Act Congress: Met in New York City in October 1765.
- Delegates from nine colonies issued a series of documents.
  1. A "Declaration of the Rights and Grievances of the Colonies" was adopted.
  2. A petition for relief was sent to George III.
  3. An appeal was addressed to Parliament to repeal the Stamp Act.
- A distinction was again drawn between imperial *regulatory* laws (permissible) and internal *taxation* (objectionable).
- American merchants organized nonimportation associations to apply pressure on Britain's economy.

Repeal of the Stamp Act: By Parliament in March 1766.
- Followed another change of ministers in London.
- In the parliamentary debate, Edmund Burke and others spoke sympathetically of the colonists' plight.
- The **Declaratory Act**, passed at the same time, affirmed Parliament's power to pass laws affecting the colonies "in all cases whatsoever" but did not specifically mention taxes.

KEY QUOTATION

Pro Patria
The first Man that Either distributes or makes use of Stampt Paper let him take care of his House, Person and Effects.
Vox Populi
We dare!

New York City poster, October 1765

Key 16   The crisis deepens (1766–74)

OVERVIEW *The British government's efforts to tighten controls on the colonies and to raise revenue by various taxes met with growing resistance from American radicals hastening the drift toward revolution.*

The Townshend Acts: Passed by Parliament in 1767.
- Acts of the New York Assembly were suspended until the assembly obeyed the Quartering Act.
- Duties (external taxes) were placed on glass, lead, paint, paper, and tea (which could only be legally imported from England).
- Customs (tariff) administration was now to be centered in Boston.
- Money raised would pay governors and other English officials, independent of colonial legislatures.

Resistance to new taxes: Mounted again.
- **John Dickinson**'s *Letters of a Pennsylvania Farmer,* objecting to all forms of taxes for revenue, were widely distributed.
- The governor dissolved the Massachusetts legislature after it circulated a protesting *Circular Letter.*
- Sons of Liberty and Daughters of Liberty organized protests and helped enforce *nonimportation* boycotts against English imports.
- Growing mob action divided colonial opinion.
- Additional British troops were sent to Boston (1768).

Boston Massacre (March 1770): Occurred when British troops fired on a mob.
- **Crispus Attucks,** an escaped slave, was one of the first to die.
- Defended by **John Adams,** all but two soldiers were acquitted.

Parliament: With **Lord North** now heading the government, Parliament *repealed* all the Townshend duties *except* the tax on tea (to emphasize Parliament's authority).
- A three-year lull in agitation followed.
- **Committees of Correspondence** provided a network for American resisters.

The Tea Act of 1773: Designed to bail out the East India Company.
- Taxes (and price) were reduced, undercutting American merchants and smugglers.
- In Boston, a *Tea Party* dumped a cargo of tea into the harbor, and resistance occurred elsewhere.
- Other "tea parties" occurred in Charleston, S.C., and Annapolis, Md.

Coercive Acts: A series of laws that colonists called "Intolerable Acts," passed by Parliament in March 1774.

- Boston port was closed until the tea was paid for.
- British officials and soldiers could be sent to England for major trials.
- A new Quartering Act brought soldiers into Boston.
- More offices were made appointive in Massachusetts, where General Thomas Gage soon became military governor.
- A separate Quebec Act set up an undemocratic government in that expanded colony and provided the Catholic Church with special privileges.
- Sympathy and assistance for Boston came from other colonies.
- Thomas Jefferson's *Summary View* argued for allegiance to the king but not to Parliament.

First Continental Congress: Met in Philadelphia in September 1774.

- Fifty-five delegates attended from twelve colonies.
- A series of resolutions and protests were adopted.
- Resolutions agreed with Parliament's right to regulate external commerce but not to regulate internal colonial affairs.
- A Continental Association was formed to boycott British imports.
- In Parliament, Burke and others spoke in favor of reconciliation.
- As royal governments collapsed, rebel *committees of safety* and congresses took over.

Second Continental Congress: Was called for May 1775.

- Lord North's Conciliatory Resolution failed to achieve a compromise.
- Parliament declared Massachusetts to be in a state of rebellion.

KEY FIGURE

Samuel Adams: A leading rebel agitator, he initiated the Committees of Correspondence, helped plan the Boston Tea Party, and as a delegate to the Continental Congress supported immediate independence.

Key 17 A struggle for men's minds

OVERVIEW *In providing ideological justification for revolution and in arousing public support for independence, the writings of Tom Paine and Thomas Jefferson proved to be stirring and effective.*

Colonial attitudes: Colonial protesters, who claimed all the political rights of English subjects, blamed Parliament for imposing taxes and restrictions without colonial representation.
- Several petitions to King George III from his "loyal subjects" had gone unanswered.
- Paine's January 1776 pamphlet *Common Sense* was extraordinarily popular. It argued that the colonists were exploited by Britain, made a villain of the king, and called for an independent republic.

Second Continental Congress: Met in May 1776; urged states to form their own governments.
- **Richard Henry Lee's Resolutions** (adopted July 2) stated that the Colonies "are and of right ought to be free and independent states."
- Recognizing the importance of "the opinions of mankind" at home and abroad, a committee of Benjamin Franklin, John Adams, and Thomas Jefferson drafted a "declaration."

Jefferson's Declaration of Independence: Has remained a primary source of American ideals.
- Inspiration was derived from the English Revolution of 1688 and from Enlightenment writers such as Locke and Hume.
- The Declaration recognized *natural* (inalienable) *rights* ("life, liberty, and the pursuit of happiness"), the *compact theory* ("consent of the governed"), and the *right of revolution* against tyrannical governments.
- Twenty-seven grievances (of varying validity) were enumerated, with blame placed on the king ("He has..."). At the time, these were the main focus of attention.
- An attack on slavery and the slave trade was omitted on the insistence of some Southerners.
- Recognizing the risks of "treason" ("we mutually pledge to each other our lives, our fortunes and our sacred honor"), the signers endorsed the status of "Free and Independent States."
- The Second Continental Congress accepted the document on July 4.

Key 18   Lexington to Saratoga

OVERVIEW *Revolutionary fighting began fifteen months before independence was declared. At first the fighting was primarily in the North.*

Fighting begins: First shots were fired in April 1775.
- London ordered General Gage to arrest rebel leaders **John Hancock** and **Sam Adams** and seize arms and ammunition around Boston.
- British troops planned a secret march to Concord but **Paul Revere** and others spread the alarm.
- Colonial militia (Minutemen) at Lexington were ordered to disperse and the first shots were fired (by whom?).
- The British marched on to the North Bridge at Concord.
- After the second clash the British were harassed on their return to Boston, which was then put under siege.

Battle of Bunker (Breed's) Hill: In June, the Americans were driven from their trenches near Charlestown, but the British suffered heavy losses.

Reactions: Congress appointed a Virginian, **George Washington**, General of the American Army.
- In August the king declared the colonies to be in rebellion.
- The British used professional armies and foreign mercenaries ("Hessians") to pacify and hold coastal cities.
- American rebels relied on guerrilla harassment and survival on home terrain.
- Americans were aided by foreign volunteers, including Lafayette, von Steuben, and Kosciuszko.

Canada: Refused an offer to join the Americans and resisted their invasion.
- In May 1775 Ethan Allen's "Green Mountain Boys" captured Fort Ticonderoga and its cannons, which were hauled to Boston.
- Arnold and Montgomery launched attacks on Montreal (which fell) and Quebec (which did not).

New York and New Jersey campaigns: The British evacuated Boston and landed in New York City.
- Washington was defeated at Brooklyn Heights and then in Manhattan and the Americans fled through New Jersey to Pennsylvania (low point of the war).

- Washington attacked the British at Trenton and Princeton.
- Howe's British army occupied Philadelphia and Washington's army wintered (1777–78) at Valley Forge.

Britain's strategy: To secure New York's Hudson River, cutting off New England.
- General Burgoyne took Ticonderoga (1777) and moved on Albany.
- British and Indian troops clashed with Americans on the Mohawk River and returned to Canada.
- Instead of driving up the Hudson, Howe left for Philadelphia (see above).
- Burgoyne "surrendered" to the Americans at Saratoga, N.Y. (the war's most decisive battle).
- The **Saratoga** victory helped bring France into the war as an ally (two 1778 treaties). A civil war had become an international conflict.

KEY QUOTATION

These are the times that try men's souls.

Tom Paine, *The Crises* (#1)
December, 1776 read to the
assembled troops at
Morristown, N.J.

Key 19 Revolution in the West, at sea, and in the South

OVERVIEW *After Saratoga the war stalled in the North, and focus shifted to the West and South, where the final fighting occurred.*

The West: George Rogers Clark led militia and French volunteers down the Ohio River and took several British forts.
- In response to Indian and Loyalist attacks in northeastern Pennsylvania, the Sullivan Expedition burned Iroquois villages in western New York.
- In Virginia and the Carolinas, retaliation by colonial militia devastated Cherokee Indian towns.
- Frontier counterattacks helped open land west of the Alleghenies to migration.

At sea: The Royal Navy blockaded the American coast with fair success, raiding towns and supplying British troops.
- American *privateers* (legalized raiders) harassed the British.
- The small American navy was no match for the British fleet.
- Captain **John Paul Jones** attacked British ships in their home waters. Minor skirmishes helped raise American morale and prestige.
- The French fleet provided crucial aid to the Americans.
- Britain had to also now face the Spanish and Dutch fleets.

The South: Georgia was occupied by British forces (1778) and their Southern campaign was launched.
- By May 1780 General Clinton's British expedition had taken Charleston, South Carolina.
- Banastre Tarleton's cavalry and Loyalist troops fought savage campaigns in the Carolinas against Americans under Nathanael Greene and the Swamp Fox, Francis Marion.
- While the Americans lost individual battles, Southern militia finally confined British control to coastal cities.

Yorktown: The site of the British defeat that effectively ended the war.
- Cornwallis's British army headed north to Virginia (1781).
- Admiral de Grasse's French fleet and troops left the West Indies and arrived at Chesapeake Bay.
- General Washington abandoned the siege of New York and,

accompanied by Rochambeau's French army, trapped Cornwallis on the Yorktown peninsula.

- **Cornwallis** surrendered to American and French forces (October 19, 1781).
- Scattered fighting continued for over a year.

Treaty of Paris (1783): With military difficulties elsewhere and a change in government, Britain initiated peace talks.

- American envoys (Benjamin Franklin, John Adams, and John Jay) abandoned the French alliance and signed a separate peace.
- Treaty terms recognized American independence, borders to the Mississippi (ignoring Indian claims), and fishing rights off Newfoundland.
- American promises regarding debt payment and treatment of Loyalists were not fulfilled. The British government compensated Loyalists for some damage claims.
- The American Army was almost completely disbanded.
- Washington took leave of his officers at Fraunces's Tavern in New York City and then resigned his commission as Commander.

Key 20 A social revolution?

OVERVIEW *The American War for Independence, unlike the French Revolution, did not destroy a titled aristocracy but did have a significant social impact on certain population groups.*

Feudal institutions: While few in number in America, were eliminated during the Revolution. States abolished primogeniture and entail laws.

Loyalists: An estimated one-fifth to one-third of the population remained loyal to Britain ("Tories"). Another group fluctuated with the fortunes of war or was neutral.
- Loyalists included Anglican clergymen, some religious minorities, many government officials, and some wealthy merchants.
- Some served in the British army.
- At the war's end some Loyalists' properties were seized and many Loyalists scattered to other parts of the British Empire (primarily to Nova Scotia). The result was a limited social leveling.

African-Americans: Slave and free faced a paradox. The Revolution was fought in the name of liberty and equality, but slavery continued.
- An estimated 5,000 blacks (mostly New England freemen) served in the army and navy and fought in every major battle.
- Fear of possible slave revolts inhibited use of blacks in the South.
- In 1775, Governor Dunmore of Virginia offered freedom to slaves who fled and joined the British army—as perhaps 2,000 did.
- Slavery virtually ended in the North during the Revolutionary era.

Native Americans: The protection offered by the Proclamation Line of 1763 ended with the Revolution, after which Native Americans were subjected to additional incursions on their lands.

Women: Failed to attain the status implied by the revolution's ideals, though Abigail Adams and a few others bravely challenged the lack of female equality.
- Wives often followed troops and occasionally were involved in combat.
- In absence of men, wives took on new occupations and responsibilities.

Theme 4   CONFEDERATION AND CONSTITUTION

*I*ndependence made necessary the establishment of new state and national governments. Eleven states drew up new constitutions; Connecticut and Rhode Island revised colonial charters. The Articles of Confederation created a loose union of near-sovereign states. When its achievements appeared to be outweighed by its failures, a constitutional convention wrote a new document providing for a stronger central government. Inclusion of a number of compromises and the pledge to add a Bill of Rights as amendments to protect individual liberties aided in securing ratification of the new Constitution. An important principle included in the First Amendment is freedom of religion.

INDIVIDUAL KEYS IN THIS THEME

21 New governments

22 Confederation achievements

23 Weaknesses of the Confederation

24 Constitutional Convention

25 The Constitution approved

26 Religious toleration, religious freedom

Key 21 New governments

OVERVIEW *The war for independence from Britain necessitated creation of new governments for the American states as well as for the "states assembled."*

New state constitutions: Replaced colonial charters at the urging of the Continental Congress, beginning in 1776.
- Experience with British rule caused those who drafted written constitutions to limit government power, particularly that of the governor.
- Property requirements for voting were lowered in most states and the legislatures' powers were expanded.
- Religious tests to hold office were generally retained.
- Most constitutions contained a bill of rights to protect citizens against government tyranny.
- Pennsylvania's 1776 constitution was the most radically democratic, with a one-house legislature and no governor.
- Constitutions were submitted to the people for ratification.
- Some state constitutions (notably Pennsylvania's) were rewritten in the 1780s, shifting power from legislatures to governors.

First Continental Congress: Delegates elected by colonial conventions met in Philadelphia beginning in September 1774 (see Key 16).

Second Continental Congress (1775–81): Became, in effect, the unified government for the Revolution, with most power remaining with the states.
- Congress created the Continental Army with George Washington as Commander.
- Currency was printed to pay for supplies.
- A committee was organized to deal with foreign policy.
- The Declaration of Independence was approved (see Key 17).
- A committee headed by **John Dickinson** was appointed in 1776 to write a Constitution (the Articles of Confederation).

Articles of Confederation: Adopted by the Continental Congress in 1777 and sent to the states for ratification (not achieved until 1781).
- The Articles (the first Constitution) created a loose confederation of sovereign states ("a firm league of friendship").
- Each state delegation was given one vote in the one-house Congress.
- Important legislation required a two-thirds vote of the states; a unanimous vote of state legislatures was required to amend.

Key 22   Confederation achievements

OVERVIEW *The Articles of Confederation, a transition to a stronger constitution, achieved its most important success in the handling of western lands.*

Administration of government: Through committees of Congress.
- Departments of Post Office, Finance, War, and Foreign Affairs were created.
- Robert Morris, Superintendent of Finance, attempted to stabilize tax, currency, and debt policies but was frustrated by the states.
- Confederation delegates successfully concluded the Treaty of Paris (1783), ending the Revolutionary War.

Western land claims: Long a source of dispute.
- Seven states had huge western land claims (some overlapping) based on colonial charters, while six jealous states had none.
- Indian claims to land were either ignored or overridden by a variety of treaties.
- Ratification of the Articles was delayed (by Maryland and others) until western lands were ceded to the nation "for the common benefit."
- Sale of the lands would provide a source of national revenue.

The Land Ordinance of 1785: Provided that the Old Northwest (north of the Ohio River) was to be surveyed and sold to help pay the national debt.
- Townships would be divided into 36 one-square-mile sections to be sold for a minimum of one dollar per acre.
- Income from the sale of one section was to go to the support of public schools (the first example of federal aid to education).
- Later, smaller plots at lower prices reduced land speculation.

The Northwest Ordinance (1787): Provided government for the territory.
- At first Congress would govern through appointed governors, with gradual increase in self-government (an elected legislature).
- When population permitted, three to five states could enter the union on an equal basis with the original thirteen; permanent colonial status was rejected.
- A Bill of Rights protected freedom of religion, jury trials, and other rights.
- Slavery was abolished in the territory.

Key 23   Weaknesses of the Confederation

OVERVIEW *In what some have called "the critical period," weaknesses in the Confederation seemed to prove the need to increase the power of the national government.*

The structure of government: Proved to be defective and inadequate under the Articles of Confederation. Congress could:
- Request funds and borrow money but not lay taxes or collect tariffs
- Declare war but not raise armies
- Not regulate interstate commerce
- Negotiate treaties but lacked authority abroad

Diplomatic problems: Multiplied after the war.
- Congress was unable to compel states to repay prewar debts to British citizens and allow Loyalists to recover confiscated property, as provided in the Treaty of Paris.
- European governments closed off American trade with their colonies, yet British goods flooded the American market.
- Secretary of Foreign Affairs **John Jay** negotiated a trade treaty with Spain, but it was blocked by Congress.

Financial problems: Also troubled the Confederation government.
- Congress and the states had printed "good faith" paper currency during the war. It became virtually worthless and was never redeemed.
- The Confederation government sank deeper into debt.
- Inflation reached 200% between 1776 and 1783.
- States attempted to impose their own tariffs on domestic and foreign trade.
- Foreign trade, disrupted by the war, went through a period of readjustment.

Newburgh Conspiracy (1783): George Washington successfully blocked this threatened military coup aimed at strengthening the central government and guaranteeing back pay and pensions to officers as the war came to a close.

Paxton Boys: Pennsylvania recruits, marched on Philadelphia demanding back pay and causing Congress to flee to various other cities.

Shays's Rebellion (1786): Dramatized the government's apparent inability to maintain domestic peace.

- Debtor farmers demanded more paper currency, postponement of debt and tax payments, and an end to mortgage foreclosures.
- In Rhode Island a debtor-controlled government issued a flood of paper money.
- In western Massachusetts rebel farmers led by **Daniel Shays** attempted to interrupt the operation of the courts.
- An armed band marched on the federal arsenal at Springfield.
- The rebellion was easily crushed, but fears of anarchy grew among the wealthy.

Delegates from Maryland and Virginia: Met at Mount Vernon at George Washington's invitation (March 1785) hoping to ease Potomac River and Chesapeake Bay commerce and they invited all states to send delegates to a convention at Annapolis.

Annapolis Convention (September 1786): A meeting on commercial problems, but delegates from only five states attended.
- Among the leading delegates were Alexander Hamilton, James Madison, and John Dickinson.
- Hamilton authored a resolution which called for a Philadelphia convention the next year "to render the constitution of the Federal Government adequate to the (needs) of the Union."

Key 24   Constitutional Convention

OVERVIEW *At the Constitutional Convention the Founding Fathers formulated a new document that greatly enhanced the powers of the national government.*

Philadelphia Convention: Fifty-five delegates from twelve states (Rhode Island was absent) met in the summer of 1787 for the "sole and express purpose of revising the Articles of Confederation."
- Nearly all delegates were well-educated, prosperous men of property.
- **George Washington** lent his prestige as president (chairman).
- **James Madison** ("Father of the Constitution"), a philosopher of governments, kept a journal of the sessions.
- Aging **Benjamin Franklin** contributed a moderating influence.
- Leading Revolutionary leaders were absent: John Adams and Thomas Jefferson were serving as diplomats abroad, for example.
- It was agreed that a stronger central government was necessary to restrain natural human selfishness.
- Sessions were closed to the public.

Virginia Plan: Madison's plan for a government under a new constitution was presented for him by **Edmund Randolph**.
- The "large states" plan provided for a two-house legislature with representation based on population.
- A national judiciary and an executive chosen by Congress would be created.
- Congress (and the national government) were given increased powers.

New Jersey ("small states") plan: Proposed by **William Paterson**, provided for revision of the Articles, retaining equal representation for all states in Congress.

The Great Compromise: After agreeing to scrap the Articles and write a new document, the delegates resolved the dispute over representation by accepting a proposal from **Roger Sherman** of Connecticut:
- A Senate would have all states equally represented.
- A House of Representatives would have seats allotted according to population.

Three-fifths Compromise: Borrowing from a proposed amendment to the Articles of Confederation, it was agreed that slaves would be counted at "three-fifths" for purposes of representation in Congress and for direct taxation. The foreign slave trade was not to be banned for twenty years (the word "slave" does not appear in the Constitution).

Federal system: Created in the Constitution, it divided power between national and state governments.

Separation of power: Three branches (executive, legislative, and judicial) were linked with a system of "checks and balances" to prevent any one branch from becoming too powerful.
- The president (with Washington as respected model) would have important powers as commander-in-chief of the armed forces, would control foreign policy, and would have a veto power over legislation. He would see that the laws were carried out.
- The enumerated powers of Congress (including power to tax and to regulate interstate commerce) were enhanced by a "necessary and proper" clause. Congress would have the power to impeach the president and judges and remove them from office.
- Judicial review by federal courts was implied (see Key 32).
- To curb a possible "excess of democracy," the Senate and the President were to be indirectly elected (the latter by an electoral college).
- A complex system for amending the Constitution was devised with ratification of amendments requiring approval of three-fourths (rather than all) of the states.

Ratification: After seventeen weeks all but three of the 42 delegates still present signed the document, which was then sent to the states for ratification. It was specified that it would go into effect when two-thirds, or 9 of the 13 states, had approved.

KEY QUOTATION

We the people of the United States, in order to form a more perfect union, establish justice, insure domestic tranquility, provide for the common defense, promote the general welfare, and secure the blessings of liberty to ourselves and our posterity....

Preamble to the Constitution

Key 25   The Constitution approved

OVERVIEW *The controversy over ratification of "The Second Constitution" created supportive and opposing political factions and produced the most influential analysis championing the new government,* The Federalist Papers.

Ratification of the new constitution: By special conventions since it was felt state legislatures would resist reduction in their power.

States: Despite objections that the convention had exceeded its authority, the Confederation Congress submitted the new constitution to the states.
- **Delaware** was the first state to ratify, with New Hampshire becoming the necessary ninth state in June 1788.
- In some states (Massachusetts, New York) the convention vote was very close.
- Two large states (Virginia and New York) were slow to ratify.
- North Carolina and Rhode Island, two individualistic and democratic states, were the last to ratify.

Supporters of the new constitution: Assumed the name "Federalists" and branded their opponents "Anti-Federalists."

The Federalist: A collection of 85 essays by **Alexander Hamilton**, **James Madison**, and **John Jay**.
- Using Publius as the author's name, the essays appeared in New York newspapers, helping to secure that state's ratification.
- The essays stressed the specific advantages of the new government. *Example:* In #10, Madison argued that the size of the new republic would prevent any one faction (special interest) from becoming dominant.

Anti-Federalist essays: By "Cato," "Brutus," "The Federalist Farmer," and others; appeared in newspapers and were widely reprinted. They stressed democratic reliance on state and local government.

Opposition: Also based on the Constitution's lack of a bill of rights protecting individuals from potential government tyranny.
- Early in 1788 Federalists proposed adding nine amendments, one stressing reserved powers of the states.
- The First Congress submitted twelve amendments to the states (September 1789). (see Key 27)

Key 26   Religious toleration, religious freedom

OVERVIEW *Religious belief and practice, always powerful forces in American life, came to be separated and protected from the power of the state.*

Religious dissenters: Seeking freedom to practice their beliefs, they were among the important early European settlers in the New World (see Keys 4–7).
- Some colonies, such as Penn's Quaker "Holy Experiment" were established as refuges for religious dissenters.
- New York accepted French Huguenots (Protestants) after 1685, some Sephardic Jews and many others ("a multiplicity of sects").
- While church-state ties (Puritan in New England; Church of England in the South) remained strong, the unorthodox were usually able to find sanctuary, in part because of the vastness of territory.
- Lord Baltimore, proprietor of the Maryland Colony, was a Roman Catholic. To protect this minority from a Protestant majority, the assembly passed a **Toleration Act** (1649) for all "Trinitarians" (Christians).

The Great Awakening: A series of evangelical revivals occurred during the 1730s–60s.
- It grew out of concern over the Enlightenment stress on reason. The frontier provided fertile ground for conversions.
- In western Massachusetts in the 1730s, Congregationalist minister **Jonathan Edwards** stirred his congregation with fiery sermons (such as "Sinners in the Hands of an Angry God") but also wrote learned theological studies.
- Several new "log" colleges were established.
- English Methodist **George Whitefield** made several tours of America preaching to large audiences and converting many (who were "born again").
- Other emotional itinerant preachers upset traditionalists and divided churches between Old Lights and New Lights.
- Growth of Methodist, Baptist, and other denominations underscored the importance of toleration of religious diversity.

Impact of the Enlightenment: While much of the Newtonian scientific revolution and stress on reason were acceptable to established religions, deism influenced many of the Founding Fathers (deists saw God as a remote Creator). Others, such as the English immigrant scientist Joseph Priestley, followed Unitarian beliefs.

During the American Revolution: Religious toleration began to evolve into religious freedom.
- The Anglican Church, which was closely tied to the Crown and to Loyalists, was disestablished in five colonies.
- The Virginia Declaration of Rights (1776) guaranteed religious freedom in that state.

Following the Revolution: A number of churches were "nationalized."
- The American Methodists organized in Baltimore (1784).
- In 1789 the separated Anglican Church in America was renamed Episcopal.
- In 1790 John Carroll was named the first American Roman Catholic bishop.
- New England, with its Puritan tradition, was slower to disestablish the Congregational Church (Massachusetts was the last to do so in 1833).
- Religious requirements for holding political office lingered in some states and localities.

Legislation: Religious freedom became established by law.
- James Madison's *Memorial and Remonstrance Against Religious Assessments* (1785) successfully argued against legislation in Virginia that would have raised a tax to pay teachers of religion.
- The *Virginia Statute of Religious Freedom*, authored by Thomas Jefferson, was adopted in 1786.
- The *First Amendment to the Constitution,* adopted in 1791, prohibits Congress from establishing a religion or "prohibiting the free exercise thereof."

KEY QUOTATION

All men shall be free to profess, and by argument to maintain, their opinions in matters of religion.

Thomas Jefferson, *Virginia Statute of Religious Freedom*, 1786

Theme 5   THE FEDERALIST ERA

*T*he administration of President Washington established numerous precedents as it created a government under the provisions of the federal Constitution. Alexander Hamilton helped establish a strong national economic system. Domestic tranquility was assured and efforts were made to gain respect internationally. Basic policy differences between the Federalists and the Jeffersonian Republicans resulted in the emergence of two rival political parties. Conflict with France caused domestic problems for Washington's successor. The appointment of John Marshall as Chief Justice before President John Adams left office assured continuation of Federalist philosophies in Supreme Court decisions.

INDIVIDUAL KEYS IN THIS THEME

Key 27 Establishing the new government

OVERVIEW *The skeleton of the Constitution was fleshed out by the First Congress and by the precedents set by the first president.*

The new government: The First Congress under the new Constitution had to wait a month for a quorum. **George Washington** was unanimously elected president by the electoral college. **John Adams**, with the second highest vote, became vice president.
- Congress created executive departments and Washington appointed the first members of his cabinet: State, Thomas Jefferson; Treasury, Alexander Hamilton; War, Henry Knox; Attorney General, Edmund Randolph (became part of cabinet later).
- The **Judiciary Act of 1789** established a six-member Supreme Court (appointed by the president), district courts, and three circuit courts of appeal.
- Congress submitted twelve amendments to the states, of which ten were ratified (The **Bill of Rights**, 1791). These were believed to be necessary protections of individual rights from the newly enhanced power of the national government.

Washington: Took the oath of office in New York City on April 30, 1789 after a triumphant eight-day journey from Mount Vernon. Many of his actions set important precedents.
- To bring dignity and respect to the office, Washington stressed symbolic ceremony, including regular levees, or receptions. Yet after lengthy debate Congress settled on the title of office as simply, "Mr. President."
- Washington relied on advice from his cabinet (see above) considerably beyond what had been specified or implied by the Constitution.
- Washington minimized the role of the vice president, and that office gained little stature thereafter.
- When the Senate demanded relevant documents regarding a treaty with the Creek Indians, Washington angrily refused, thus establishing the principle of executive privilege and setting limits to the Constitutional provision on *advice and consent.*
- Washington used his veto power only twice in eight years.
- In spurning a third term, Washington established a tradition not broken until 1940 (but now constitutionalized by the Twenty-second Amendment).

Key 28   Hamilton's financial plan

OVERVIEW *Secretary of the Treasury Alexander Hamilton formulated an economic plan that would help consolidate national power and advance a mercantile and industrial economy.*

Hamilton's "Report on Public Credit": Recommended that Congress pay foreign debts in full, fund the national debt (largely war bonds) at face value to actual holders (the bonds had been selling at discount), and assume state debts as a national obligation.

Debt: Hamilton felt the increased debt, by securing the support of creditors, could be a "national blessing"; Jeffersonians objected to the profits speculators would make and to the nationalistic tendencies of this far-reaching program.

Sectional feeling: Was aroused since Northern states had greater indebtedness. A compromise was reached: Southern support for "assumption" in exchange for locating a new national capital on the banks of the Potomac.

National bank: Chartering a national bank was recommended in another report and caused a stormy debate. The proposed bank would hold government funds, circulate a uniform national currency, and lend money to the government.
- Jefferson and Madison argued that the Constitution made no provision for establishing a bank ("strict construction").
- Within the cabinet debate, Hamilton successfully argued that the bank was "necessary and proper" to perform the government's financial functions ("loose construction").
- Congress approved a 20-year charter for the "Bank of the United States."

Taxes: Raising revenue and encouraging American manufacturing were the subjects of a third report.
- The complex plan for support of industry was the only Hamiltonian proposal Congress rejected (manufacturing interests were not yet strong or influential enough).
- Hamilton managed to get only modest tariff rates (not yet *protective*).
- Congress approved the proposal for an excise tax on whiskey. This tax would fall hardest on Western farmers.

The Whiskey Rebellion (1794): Western Pennsylvania farmers, who relied on selling their distilled grain, rose in defiance of the excise tax.

- A strong militia force (led by General Henry Lee and Alexander Hamilton) easily scattered the "rebels."
- The incident confirmed the power of the national government to enforce its laws.
- For most Westerners this provided additional reasons to support the Jeffersonian opposition.

Hamilton's program: Established a tradition of national government support of commercial capitalism. Opponents protested that it favored a particular class (wealthy, industrial, mercantile) and a section (the Northeast).

KEY QUOTATIONS

The incorporation of a bank, and the powers assumed by this bill have not, in my opinion, been delegated to the United States by the Constitution.

Thomas Jefferson

There are implied as well as express(ed) powers and the former are as effectively delegated as the latter.

Alexander Hamilton
(from letters to President Washington
on the Constitutionality of a
U.S. Bank)

Key 29   Foreign policy under Washington

OVERVIEW *Despite attempts to maintain American commerce and neutrality, the Washington Administration became tangled in Europe's turmoil.*

The French Revolution: Presented problems for the Washington Administration.
- Initial American approval soured after the execution of the French king and queen and after the Reign of Terror began.
- Britain and France began two decades of almost uninterrupted war (1793–1815).
- America's alliance with France (Treaty of 1778) was to have been "forever."
- The American economy relied, however, on trade with Britain and that country was attempting to halt profitable American trade with the French West Indies.

Citizen Edmond Genêt: Minister (ambassador) from the revolutionary French government, landed in South Carolina, a Jeffersonian stronghold.
- Overestimating public sympathy for the Revolution, he directly recruited active American support for France.
- Washington demanded Genêt's recall.
- The embarrassing affair (underscoring foreign policy differences within the Washington administration) led to a neutrality proclamation.

Neutrality Proclamation (1793): Washington proclaimed official neutrality in Europe's conflict and admonished United States citizens to be impartial. In reality, United States isolation from Europe's quarrels proved impossible to achieve.

Northwest Territory: American frontiersmen were attacked by Indians, who were encouraged by the British in Canada.
- General Arthur St. Clair's American militia suffered a major defeat at the hands of the Indians (1791).
- After an expedition under General "Mad Anthony" Wayne defeated the Indians at the **Battle of Fallen Timbers** (1794), the tribes were forced by terms of the Treaty of Greenville (1795) to sell off large areas North of the Ohio River.

Jay's Treaty: John Jay, the Chief Justice on special mission to Great Britain, negotiated a commercial treaty (November 1794).

- Britain agreed to ease trade restrictions and abandon western forts.
- Several topics were referred to arbitration.
- The treaty also made concessions that raised a storm of opposition in the United States (Britain refused to abandon impressment).
- After a close Senate vote of approval (June 1795), Washington signed the treaty.

Pinckney's Treaty (1795): Spain, fearing better relations between Britain and the United States, agreed to American terms.
- Navigation rights on the Mississippi River were approved.
- Spain gave up claim to a large area north of Florida.

Washington's Farewell Address (1796): Largely authored by Hamilton, and published in newspapers, it deplored sectionalism and "partisan strife" (see Key 30).
- The outgoing president approved of commercial but not political ties abroad.
- He recommended that permanent alliances (such as the one with France) should be avoided and the United States should follow an independent foreign policy.
- This "advice" was recalled for a century and a half by isolationists who tended to oversimplify or misinterpret Washington's message.

KEY QUOTATION

The great rule of conduct for us in regard to foreign nations is, in extending our commercial relations to have with them as little political connection as possible.

George Washington, *Farewell Address*

Key 30   A two-party system

OVERVIEW   *While Washington deplored the "spirit of party" in his* Farewell Address *opposition political factions were creating the two-party system.*

Political parties: Factions were condemned by the Founding Fathers because they would endanger national unity. The Constitution makes no mention of political parties, which are, therefore, extra-constitutional.

Causes: Basic differences in philosophy and objectives gradually led to formulation of two factions: the Federalists, led by Alexander Hamilton and John Adams, and the Republicans, led by James Madison and Thomas Jefferson.

KEY DIFFERENCES

Federalists
- Favored strong central government
- "Loose" interpretation of the Constitution
- Encouragement of commerce and manufacturing
- Strongest in Northeast
- Favored close ties with Britain
- Emphasized order and stability

Republicans
- Emphasized states' rights
- "Strict" interpretation
- Preference for agriculture and rural life
- Strength in South and West
- Foreign policy sympathized with France
- Stressed civil liberties and trust in the people

(In practice, these generalizations were often blurred and sometimes contradicted.)

Washington's administration: President Washington attempted to discourage or mediate differences within his administration. However, growing disputes with Hamilton helped lead to Jefferson's resignation from the cabinet (1793).

In 1796: Congressional caucuses chose John Adams and Thomas Pinckney (of South Carolina) as Federalist candidates and Thomas Jefferson and Aaron Burr (of New York) as Republican candidates (sectional balance of tickets may already be seen).

Key 31   The Adams administration

OVERVIEW *President John Adams was preoccupied with an undeclared war with France and with a related domestic civil liberties crisis. Adams inherited Washington's policy problems but not his aura of leadership.*

1796 Presidential election:
- Each elector cast two ballots, with the second highest vote-getter becoming vice president.
- John Adams was elected president but some Federalists split their votes, and Thomas Jefferson, his opponent, ran second and became vice president.
- President Adams immediately faced serious foreign policy problems.

X, Y, Z Affair: France, angered by Jay's Treaty and America's apparent abandonment of the 1778 Alliance, began seizing American ships. Seeking to avoid war, Adams sent three negotiators to Paris.
- Three agents (referred to as "X, Y, and Z" by Adams) of Talleyrand, the French Foreign Minister, demanded bribes.
- Congress and the American press were angered ("Millions for defense but not one cent for tribute!").
- The Department of the Navy was created and ships were feverishly built.

Threat of war: Undeclared naval warfare with France continued for over two years (1798–1800), chiefly in the West Indies. Adams successfully resisted the public clamor for a declaration of war, however.
- The Convention of 1800, negotiated with Napoleon's new government, terminated the Alliance of 1778 (the last for the United States for a century and a half).
- The United States agreed to give up claims for indemnity for shipping losses.

Alien and Sedition Acts (1798): The Federalist-controlled Congress passed laws that would cripple the "disloyal" Republicans.
- A Naturalization Act lengthened the residence requirement for aliens (considered likely to vote Republican) to become citizens.
- Two Alien Acts (never enforced) authorized detention or deportation of "dangerous" aliens.
- A Sedition Act provided for restrictions on free speech and free-

dom of the press; ten outspoken Jeffersonian editors were convicted of "defaming" the government.

Virginia and Kentucky Resolutions (1798): With judicial review not yet established, Republicans turned to state legislatures to oppose the Alien and Sedition Acts.
- Madison, for Virginia, and, secretly, Vice President Jefferson, for Kentucky, authored resolutions affirming the compact theory of government.
- States could *nullify* (refuse to obey) unconstitutional federal actions, the resolutions argued.

Significance: Though no other states joined the protest, the states' rights theory and nullification would be later revived, especially in the South.
- America had again been unwillingly drawn into Europe's conflicts.
- The right to dissent was (not for the last time) endangered by patriotic war enthusiasm as well as by political opportunism.

KEY QUOTATION

I desire no other inscription over my gravestone than 'Here lies John Adams, who took upon himself the responsibility of the peace with France in the year 1800.'

John Adams

Key 32 The Marshall Supreme Court

OVERVIEW *The Supreme Court, originally (according to Hamilton) the weakest and "least dangerous" branch, under Chief Justice John Marshall greatly increased its power and prestige and that of the national government.*

The Constitutional judiciary: Article II creates "one Supreme Court" and "such inferior (lesser) courts as Congress may...establish."
* Appointive life terms (dependent on good behavior) were intended to assure political independence.
* The Court's decisions rely on the executive branch for enforcement.
* Judicial review (the power to determine constitutionality) is implied (Hamilton deals with this explicitly in *Federalist #78*).

Creating the courts: The **Judiciary Act of 1789** established a six-member Supreme Court, district courts, and circuit courts of appeal. Under Chief Justice John Jay, the Supreme Court was largely inactive (see Key 27).
* *Chisholm v. Georgia* (1793) determined that states may be sued in federal courts by citizens of other states. This was overridden by the Eleventh Amendment (1798).
* *Ware v. Hylton* (1796) was the first time a state law was declared unconstitutional.

The Marshall Court (1801–35): John Marshall, a Virginia Federalist, was Adams' "midnight appointment" as Chief Justice in January 1801. Marshall dominated the Supreme Court, writing nearly half the decisions and dissenting only eight times, even after Federalists lost a majority. Thus, the Court continued to enunciate Federalist principles through the Jeffersonian Era.

Marbury v. Madison (1803): The Court was established as the arbiter of the Constitution (the principle of judicial review).
* New Secretary of State James Madison refused to deliver a justice of the peace appointment to Marbury, a Federalist.
* Marbury requested a writ of mandamus (court order to compel performance of duty).
* The Court decided that the Judiciary Act had unconstitutionally given federal courts power to issue writs of mandamus.
* Other cases reviewed and approved Congressional legislation, but no other legislation was rejected by the Court for over 50 years.

Fletcher v. Peck (1810): When the Georgia legislature attempted to void an earlier fraudulent land grant, the Court upheld property rights by ruling that the state's action would "impair the obligations of contract."

McCulloch v. Maryland (1819): National laws were given precedence over state laws. The Court ruled that:
- A state tax on the Second Bank of the United States was unconstitutional.
- A national bank is implied by the "necessary and proper" and other clauses of the Constitution.

Dartmouth College v. Woodward (1819): The Court established the sanctity of contracts. New Hampshire had attempted to take over Dartmouth College by revising its colonial charter. The Court ruled that the charter was protected under the contract clause.

Gibbons v. Ogden (1824): The Court clarified the commerce clause, affirming Congressional power over interstate commerce by overturning a New York State law that gave a monopoly of Hudson River ferry service to one company.

KEY QUOTATIONS

It is emphatically the province and duty of the judicial department to say what the law is.

John Marshall, *Marbury v. Madison*

Scarcely any question arises in the United States which does not become, sooner or later, a subject of judicial debate.

Alexis de Tocqueville, *Democracy in America*, 1835

Theme 6   THE JEFFERSONIANS

*T*he "Revolution of 1800" brought the Jeffersonian Republicans to power. Although Republicans favored decentralization and more limited national government power, their actions when in office sometimes contradicted their principles. Despite doubts on constitutionality, Jefferson doubled the territory of the United States by purchasing Louisiana from France. Efforts to avoid involvement in the Napoleonic Wars failed, and a resultant second war with Britain was inconclusive. A postwar surge of nationalism produced a compromise on slavery in the new territories and a protective doctrine for the Western Hemisphere. The death of the Federalist Party produced new political alignments.

Key 33   Jefferson in office

OVERVIEW   *In what some termed "the Revolution of 1800," political power was peacefully transferred from the Federalists to the Jeffersonian Republicans.*

Election of 1800: Federalists were hurt by intra-party feuds between Adams and Hamilton.
- Republicans **Thomas Jefferson** and **Aaron Burr** tied in electoral votes, sending the election to the Federalist-controlled "lame duck" House of Representatives.
- After 35 ballots Jefferson was chosen, in part because of Hamilton's influence (Burr became vice president). This helped lead to a duel (1804) in which Burr killed Hamilton.
- The electoral deadlock led to adoption of the Twelfth Amendment (1804), which provided for separate balloting for president and vice president.

Inaugural Address: In the new national capital, Washington, D.C., Jefferson stressed political reconciliation ("We are all Republicans, we are all Federalists").

Domestic affairs: Democratic simplicity was stressed by the new administration which initially sought to follow "republican philosophy." (See Key 30.)
- The Sedition and Naturalization Acts were allowed to lapse.
- Federal excise taxes (damaging to western farmers) were repealed.
- Secretary of the Treasury **Albert Gallatin** sought to reduce government spending and balance the budget.
- The size of both the army and navy was reduced.

Barbary Coast pirates: Continued to exact "tribute" (bribes) to spare American shipping off North Africa.
- The Pasha of Tripoli declared war on the United States (1801).
- Jefferson dispatched a naval squadron to attempt to force a settlement. This led to a peace treaty (1805).

Judiciary Act of 1801: Enabled President Adams to appoint fifteen last minute ("Midnight") Federalist judges (see Key 32).
- One Federalist district judge was impeached and removed from office by the new Republican Congress.
- An attempt to remove Supreme Court Justice Samuel Chase on partisan political grounds failed.

Key 34   The Louisiana Purchase

OVERVIEW *The most popular and far-reaching achievement of the Jefferson administration was the purchase of the Louisiana territory, which opened vast new lands and stimulated continental expansion.*

Geographical significance: The Louisiana territory defined the western border of the United States after the 1783 Treaty of Paris. The Mississippi River and New Orleans were important to Western agriculture. The United States had impulses toward territorial expansion.

History: Ceded by France to Spain after the French and Indian War (1763) (see Key 13), Louisiana was returned to France in 1800 as Napoleon sought to rebuild the French overseas empire. However, by 1802 Napoleon was running into difficulties:
- Attempts to recover Santo Domingo (Haiti) were frustrated by black troops under **Toussaint L'Ouverture** and by yellow fever.
- Caribbean bases were lost, and war with England was renewed.
- There was clamor in the United States for war with France.

Opportunity for the United States: Jefferson sent Monroe to France to help negotiate the purchase of New Orleans. Napoleon offered to sell all of Louisiana for $15 million. **Monroe** and **Livingston** signed the treaty for the purchase in April 1803.

Consequences: The purchase doubled the size of the United States at a cost of 3 cents an acre, but it presented a Constitutional dilemma:
- There was no Constitutional provision for land purchase. Some argued that an amendment was required.
- Although a strict constructionist, Jefferson promoted the purchase as a benefit to the nation.
- The Senate approved the treaty over Federalist objections.

Explorations: The Louisiana boundaries were poorly defined, and the territory was largely unknown.
- Jefferson sent an exploratory mission under **Lewis** and **Clark** (1804–06). Using Indian guides, they followed the Missouri and Columbia rivers to the Pacific Coast (Oregon), gathering geographic and scientific information.
- **Zebulon Pike** sought the source of the Mississippi and explored Colorado and New Mexico (1805–07). Travel accounts stirred commercial ambitions.
- In the 1820s the Santa Fe Trail from St. Louis was opened.

Key 35   Failure of neutrality

OVERVIEW *Renewal of warfare in Europe posed serious problems for the Jefferson and Madison administrations. Various efforts at avoiding involvement yet affirming neutral rights at sea ended in failure and a second war with Britain began in 1812.*

The Napoleonic Wars: Fighting between France and Britain was renewed in 1803.
- The United States was the largest neutral trader with both sides.
- Napoleon won a series of military victories in Europe.
- After its naval victory at Trafalgar (1805), Britain controlled the seas.
- *Orders in Council* (1804–05) attempted to impose a British blockade on the continent.
- Napoleon responded with counter-blockade decrees.
- The United States attempted to continue profitable neutral trade by "breaking" voyages (landing in American ports en route from the West Indies to France).

Provocations: Stirred American anger.
- Some American ships and cargoes were seized.
- The British navy, searching for deserters, *impressed* (seized) some American sailors.
- In 1807 a British ship fired on the USS *Chesapeake* near the Virginia coast and seized several alleged deserters.

American reaction: American attempts to affirm *neutral rights* began with an 1806 **Non-Importation Act** aimed at Britain.
- An **Embargo Act** (1807) suspending all trade actually hurt New England's commerce and Western farmers.
- The Embargo was repealed early in 1809 just before Jefferson left office.
- Two other acts under President Madison attempted to "bribe" Britain or France to stop interfering with U.S. trade.
- Napoleon "agreed" and non-intercourse was again applied to Britain.

War Hawks: Henry Clay, John C. Calhoun, and others agitated for war in the Congress.
- Westerners blamed the British for promoting new attacks by Indians on the frontier. (See Key 44.)

- Extremists clamored for conquest. ("On to Canada!") No territorial gains would be likely from a war with France.

Madison's War Message (June 1, 1812): Stressed Britain's interference with neutral shipping, impressment of sailors, and provocation of Indian attacks. National pride and expansionism were not mentioned.

Congressional division: The vote for war was fairly close (79–49 in the House) and reflected sectional and political divisions.
- Commercial states of the North, which relied on trade with Britain, opposed the war (except Pennsylvania, where Jeffersonian political loyalty prevailed).
- Southern and Western representatives (reflecting both expansionism and party loyalty) generally voted in favor of war (40–9), even though the Embargo had hurt many Western farmers.

KEY QUOTATION

The conduct of [Britain's] government presents a series of acts hostile to the United States as an independent and neutral nation.

Madison's War Message

Key 36   War of 1812

OVERVIEW *The nation was poorly prepared for war in 1812. The few American successes on the water did not compensate for failures to successfully invade Canada, and the war ended in stalemate.*

Attempts to invade Canada:
- Americans raided and burned the Canadian capital at York (Toronto), April 1813.
- On the Niagara border the United States was hampered by poor leadership and the refusal of some militia to leave their states.

Naval war: Victory in single-ship engagements heartened the Americans, but the Royal Navy controlled the Atlantic. Only privateers could elude their blockade.

Great Lakes: Control of the Great Lakes was crucial. After furious shipbuilding by both sides, **Oliver Hazard Perry** won a naval battle on Lake Erie.
- The British and their Indian allies were defeated by **William Henry Harrison** at the Battle of the Thames. (See Key 44.) **Tecumseh** was killed.

Britain: Saw renewed war with America as a frustrating minor conflict compared to its struggle with Napoleon. Napoleon's defeat and exile enabled Britain to send reenforcements to Canada and take the offensive (1814).
- A naval victory by the Americans on Lake Champlain caused an invading British force to return to Canada.
- British troops, landed below Washington, burned the capital in reprisal for the burning of York.

Andrew Jackson: Defeated Creek Indians at Horseshoe Bend.
- Jackson took Pensacola in West Florida.
- British troops sent from the West Indies were defeated when they attacked Jackson's forces (including free blacks) at New Orleans (January 8, 1815). Although occurring after the peace agreement had been signed, the battle of New Orleans gave Americans a sense of victory and speeded ratification of the treaty.

The peace treaty: Was signed at Ghent, Belgium, December 24, 1814.
- Both sides, weary of fighting, ignored the causes of the war and restored the status quo (no mention of maritime rights).

Key 37   A new nationalism

OVERVIEW *Although the War of 1812 had increased sectional disunity, the postwar period witnessed a burst of American nationalism.*

Sectionalism: The most dramatic expression during the war had been in New England.
- The war had been opposed by New England and the Middle Atlantic states.
- Despite the embargo and blockade, illegal trade continued.
- Massachusetts Federalists called for a meeting to take regional action against the war and to amend the Constitution.
- The **Hartford Convention**, a states rights protest, convened secretly in December 1815, with 22 delegates present from five New England states.
- Moderates prevailed over secession talk, but seven Constitutional amendments were proposed, aimed at crippling Republican political power.
- Stress on the "sovereignty of states and liberties of the people" echoed the Virginia and Kentucky Resolutions (see Key 31).
- Jackson's victory at New Orleans and the end of the war caused protest to fizzle.
- The Federalist Party, branded as disloyal, was seriously hurt.

Effects: Although the war was of little global importance, it had important effects at home, including:
- Reassuring American political and economic independence and gradually improving relations with Britain.
- Resolving to avoid future entanglements in European conflicts (affirmed in "Monroe Doctrine," see Key 38).
- Stirring nationalism in Canada in response to American invasion attempts.
- Weakening of Western Indian tribes, which had allied with Britain.
- Encouraging of domestic manufacturing due to decline of trade during the war.
- Emerging of war heroes as national political prospects (Andrew Jackson, William Henry Harrison) and of new regional political leaders (South: Calhoun; North: Webster; West: Clay).

Nationalistic fervor: Emerged from an indecisive war.
- With Congressional approval, an American naval squadron punished North African Barbary Coast pirates who had resumed

molesting American shipping during the war.
- Madison and the Republican Congress authorized a peacetime standing army.
- Congressman Henry Clay began to promote a program that became known as "The American System":
  1. a protective tariff
  2. a rechartered national bank
  3. national financing of transportation systems
- Economic nationalism was expressed in the chartering of the Second Bank of the United States (signed by President Madison in a reversal of Jeffersonian philosophy).
- Many Jeffersonian Republicans (including John C. Calhoun of South Carolina) supported passage of the first protective tariff (1816). Infant American industry had accused Britain of dumping cheap goods on American markets after the war.
- However, doubting the constitutionality of using federal money to build local roads, Madison vetoed an *internal improvements* bill.

KEY FIGURE

John C. Calhoun: South Carolina's political leader supported the national bank and a nationalistic protective tariff in 1816 but by 1828 had become the leading proponent of Southern states' rights.

Key 38 Monroe administration

OVERVIEW *The so-called "Era of Good Feeling" of the Monroe administration (1817–25) was marred by economic depression, a resurgence of sectionalism, and gradual political realignment.*

Virginia dynasty: Continued in the person of James Monroe, last of the Revolutionary generation. (Secretaries of State tended to become the next president.)
- A discredited Federalist Party ran its last candidate for president in 1816 (Monroe's first election).
- In 1820 Monroe was unopposed for reelection, winning all electoral votes but one.

Panic of 1819: Brought on three years of economic depression.
- Post-war expansion had been fed by over-extension of credit by banks and speculation in western land.
- As cotton prices fell, Southern planters criticized the protective tariff.
- Western farmers blamed the Second Bank of the United States for tightening the money supply.
- A new Land Act (1820) reduced size and price for acquiring land from the government.

Slavery: In the territories revealed sectional tensions.
- Congress abolished the importation of slaves as of January 1, 1808.
- In 1819 Missouri applied for admission as a slave state. This would upset the balance of free and slave states (eleven each).
- The Tallmadge amendment providing for a ban on further introduction of slaves and gradual emancipation in Missouri was accepted by the House but was rejected by the Senate.

Henry Clay's Missouri Compromise (1820): The deadlock in Congress was broken by compromises.
- Slavery would be prohibited in the Louisiana territory north of 36°30′.
- Missouri, though north of the line, would come in as a slave state.
- With permission from Massachusetts, Maine would be admitted as a separate free state to maintain the balance in the Senate.
- The compromise nearly failed over Missouri's efforts to exclude free blacks.

Key 39   A nationalist foreign policy

OVERVIEW   *Postwar nationalism was reflected in efforts to expand and secure the country's borders and in attempts to insulate the Western Hemisphere from Europe's conflicts.*

John Quincy Adams: Was President Monroe's capable Secretary of State (1817–25).
- The **Rush-Bagot Treaty** with Britain (1817) limited Great Lakes fleets and demilitarized the border with Canada.
- The Convention of 1818 defined the border with Canada as the 49th parallel from Minnesota to Oregon and provided for joint occupation of Oregon for ten years. Joint fishing rights off Newfoundland were also agreed to.
- General Andrew Jackson pursued "outlaw" Seminole Indians into Florida (1818). The Florida "panhandle" had been annexed between 1810 and 1813.
- Faced with its likely loss, Spain ceded East Florida to the U.S. in the **Adams-Onis Treaty** (1819). The western borders of Louisiana were defined so as to not include Texas.

Europe and America: Following the defeat of Napoleon in 1815, the allies, meeting at the Congress of Vienna, attempted to restore the prewar status quo.
- The Concert of Europe attempted to bolster conservative European monarchies and their control over colonies abroad, including in Latin America.
- Wars of liberation freed Latin America from Spanish control (1808–22).
- U.S. recognition was extended to new republics (1822–26), while fears of European intervention to restore colonies increased.
- Russian claims to territory from Alaska through Oregon were settled by a treaty (1824) establishing 54°40' as their southern boundary.

The Monroe Doctrine: An attempt to forestall European intervention and incursion into the Western Hemisphere.
- A growing commerce with Latin America led Great Britain to oppose colonial restoration.
- Foreign Minister Canning's proposal for a joint British-U.S. declaration was rejected by Adams.

- American policy, formulated by Adams, was stated in Monroe's last Annual Message to Congress:
    1. No additional European colonization would be tolerated in the Western Hemisphere (*non-colonization*).
    2. Monarchical systems were to stay out of the hemisphere (*non-intervention*).
    3. The U.S. would not interfere in European affairs or in their existing colonies.
- The Doctrine has no standing in international law and attracted little attention at the time, when the British navy shielded the hemisphere.
- Modified and extended later (by Presidents Polk and Theodore Roosevelt, for example), it became a centerpiece of U.S. foreign policy.

KEY QUOTATION

...we should consider any attempt on their part to extend their system to any portion of this hemisphere as dangerous to our peace and safety.

Monroe Doctrine

Key 40   Political realignments

OVERVIEW *The 1820s saw a widening of popular participation in politics and realignment of political parties.*

The Federalist Party: Virtually ceased to exist after 1816 on the national level.

Suffrage (the vote): Was gradually being expanded among adult white males as the property requirement was abandoned.
- Voter reform came first in the Western states, last in the South, and only in Rhode Island was it accompanied by any violence (Dorr Rebellion, 1843).
- The vote of the people replaced state legislatures in selecting presidential electors.

Election of 1824: The Republicans failed to agree on one nominee for president, and four factional candidates emerged. A Congressional caucus chose William Crawford (the last time this system was used); Henry Clay of Kentucky won support from Western state legislatures; Secretary of State John Quincy Adams was supported by New England; and Andrew Jackson of Tennessee enjoyed broad national support as a war hero. John C. Calhoun withdrew and became the Vice Presidential candidate.
- Jackson received the most popular votes but no one received an electoral college majority.
- As provided by the 12th Amendment, the choice (from the top 3 candidates) went to the House of Representatives.
- With the support of Clay, Adams received a majority of state votes in the House. Jackson supporters denounced the supposed "corrupt bargain" as Clay was then named Secretary of State.

President John Quincy Adams: Lacking in tact and in willingness to compromise, he faced criticism from Jacksonians throughout his term (his foes controlled Congress after the 1826 elections).
- A nationalist, Adams supported internal improvements (roads and canals) at federal expense.
- Adams expressed concern for the rights of Native Americans.
- Congress hampered the administration's plan to attend a Pan-American Conference in Panama, and Adams failed to persuade Britain to reopen its West Indies possessions to United States trade.

Theme 7   THE AGE OF JACKSON

*T*he election of Andrew Jackson in 1828 came to symbolize the emergence of a new democratic spirit: an "age of the common man." Although the Democrats favored limited national government, Jackson forcefully responded to South Carolina's defiance over the collection of tariffs. The exercise of assertive executive power is best illustrated by Jackson's veto of the rechartering of the national bank and his "war" against that "monopoly." The removal of Indian tribes from the Southeast to lands west of the Mississippi was vigorously pursued. A new Whig Party emerged in opposition to "King Andrew I."

INDIVIDUAL KEYS IN THIS THEME

41 Jacksonian democracy

42 Jackson and the Bank

43 Tariffs and nullification

44 Indian removal

45 Post-Jackson politics

Key 41   Jacksonian democracy

OVERVIEW *A widening of voter participation and the emergence of modern political party organization helped achieve the political revolution of the Jackson years.*

Election of 1828: Supporters of Adams for reelection were now called the National Republicans and Andrew Jackson's followers were known as the Democratic Republicans.
- In a mud-slinging campaign, Adams was portrayed as an aristocratic hypocrite and Jackson as an adulterer.
- Jackson's victory brought to power what his critics called "King Mob" but what the Jacksonians considered to be the symbolic political triumph of the common man.

Civil service reform: Was attempted through President Jackson's appointive power.
- Periodic rotation in office, said the Jacksonians, would reduce corruption and provide democratic opportunity.
- Critics, however, condemned Jackson's appointments, based on political loyalty, as the operation of a spoils system.
- Less than one-fifth of appointed office holders were removed.
- Jackson came to rely upon the informal advice of friends (his Kitchen Cabinet).
- Internal rivalry developed between Secretary of State **Martin Van Buren** of New York and Vice President **John C. Calhoun** of South Carolina.
- A petty scandal involving a cabinet member's wife (the "Peggy Eaton Affair") contributed to conflict within the administration.

Jeffersonian tradition: Jackson favored limited government but strengthened the presidency.
- Jackson vetoed the Maysville Road Bill (1830), calling federal funding for local improvements unconstitutional.
- Another veto blocked Henry Clay's bill to distribute to the states funds raised from the sale of public lands.
- Jackson exercised the veto twelve times—more than the six previous presidents combined. Critics and political cartoonists referred to "King Veto" and "King Andrew the First."

Chief Justice Roger B. Taney: Jackson's appointee, he ruled in *Charles River Bridge v. Warren Bridge* (1837) that the interests of the community are more important than corporate rights. This states-rights decision departed from the Marshall court's nationalism.

Key 42   Jackson and the Bank

OVERVIEW   *The chief issue in the 1832 election turned out to be Jackson's war on the U.S. Bank. The presidential veto was followed by a period of economic uncertainty and finally, a major depression.*

The Second Bank of the United States: Chartered in 1816, it was headed after 1823 by **Nicholas Biddle**. President Jackson's opposition to the Bank was shared by:
- Westerners, who preferred state and local banks and easier credit
- Debtors, who considered the Bank a financial monopoly favoring the wealthy
- States rights advocates, who considered the U.S. Bank to be unconstitutional

The Bank war: Henry Clay and Biddle sought to make the Bank an issue in the presidential election by having Congress pass a rechartering bill in 1832, four years early.
- Jackson's veto message denounced monopoly and privilege.
- The president challenged the Supreme Court's earlier decision on the Bank's constitutionality.
- Congress failed to override the veto.

Election of 1832: For the first time, party conventions were used, nominating Democrat Jackson and National Republican Henry Clay.
- Jackson interpreted his victory as a mandate to dismantle the Bank.
- Jackson had Secretary of the Treasury Taney remove federal funds and deposit them in state-chartered (pet) banks.
- These banks printed inflationary paper currency.
- The rise of state debt, a proposal to distribute surplus federal funds to the states, and speculation in Western land added to the financial crisis.

The Specie Circular (1836): Jackson, fearing paper money inflation, had the Treasury order that only specie (gold or silver) would be accepted for purchase of federal land.

Election of 1836: Jackson's hand-picked successor, **Martin Van Buren**, defeated several Whig opponents.
- The Panic of 1837 (a major depression) was popularly blamed on Jackson's bank policies (the Second Bank had died in 1836).
- At Van Buren's urging a federal subtreasury system was created, independent of state and private banks.

Key 43   Tariffs and nullification

OVERVIEW   *Emerging sectional economic differences came to focus on disputes over enactment of high protective tariffs, generating states rights opposition.*

Protective Tariff rates of 1816 (see Key 37): Were raised then again in 1824 under President Monroe. It failed to keep out British woolen imports, however.

Tariff of 1828: In an attempt to embarrass President Adams, the Jacksonians introduced a new tariff bill.
- Northern states, which were increasingly industrialized, voted for the higher rates.
- Southern members of Congress, reflecting their states' growing reliance on cotton exports and the purchase of manufactured goods, voted against the bill.
- The reversal of positions by Daniel Webster and John C. Calhoun reflected economic changes in their sections of the nation.
- Congress passed the "Tariff of Abominations," and President Adams signed it.

Opposition: South Carolina led the sectional opposition to higher tariffs.
- Vice President John C. Calhoun anonymously wrote "The South Carolina Exposition and Protest," extolling the principle of state sovereignty.
- The pamphlet branded the tariff unconstitutional and recommended nullification of the law by states that opposed it.
- In his theory of the *concurrent majority* (a sectional veto power for the minority South), Calhoun sought to protect the interests of a minority South against majority tyranny.
- No other states joined South Carolina's protest, and a nullification vote failed in its legislature.

Webster-Hayne debate (1830): Argument over public land policies developed into a classic debate between the Massachusetts and South Carolina senators over the nature of the Union.
- Robert Hayne (South Carolina) defended state sovereignty and the doctrine of nullification.
- Daniel Webster (Massachusetts) replied that the union was "one and inseparable" and that nullification was treasonable.

Tariff of 1832: Reduced rates by 10% but was still protective.
- A special South Carolina convention declared the tariff *null and*

void in that state and threatened secession (Ordinance of Nullification).

- President Jackson responded with a ringing proclamation ("Disunion by armed force is treason") and threatened to send a military force to enforce tariff collections.
- Calhoun resigned as vice president to become South Carolina's spokesman in the Senate.
- Other Southern states refused to support nullification or secession.
- Congress passed a "force bill" approving presidential military action, if necessary.
- Henry Clay's *Compromise Tariff* (for gradual rate reduction) was passed (1833). South Carolina rescinded its nullification ordinance, and the crisis subsided.

Federalism: The proper balance of national and state power and authority was the central issue of the tariff controversy.

- Northern industrial development was aided by higher, protective tariffs.
- Northern economic and population growth appeared to threaten the South's economic, political, and social systems.
- The doctrine of *nullification* restated states rights theory.
- Possible secession and disunion were averted by compromise.

KEY FIGURE

Henry Clay: one of the pre-Civil War "great triumvirate" in the Senate, he authored key compromises which postponed conflict but lost contests for the presidency three times.

Key 44   Indian removal

OVERVIEW *As settlers moved westward in search of land, a policy was sought to deal with resistant Indian tribes.*

Treaties: Continuing a colonial tradition, the United States signed many treaties with "sovereign" Indian tribes. In reality, treaties were ignored in the rush for Western land.

Indian disunity: Hampered resistance.
- Shawnee chiefs **Tecumseh** and the **Prophet** attempted, unsuccessfully, to form a confederation of Northwestern tribes.
- William Henry Harrison's troops defeated the Indians at Tippecanoe Creek (1811).
- Tecumseh was killed while fighting on the British side in the War of 1812 and the unity movement collapsed.

Indian policy: The Bureau of Indian Affairs was created in 1824 and made part of the Department of Interior in 1849.
- Agents monopolized Indian trade; economic dependency increased.
- Some attempts were made at Christianizing and educating Indians (boarding schools).
- President Monroe in 1824 urged removal of Southern tribes to protected lands west of the Mississippi, but the tribes refused.

Supreme Court: Chief Justice John Marshall in *Cherokee Nation v. Georgia* (1831) ruled that the state could not seize lands without the consent of the "domestic dependent nation," but Georgia and President Jackson both ignored the decision.

Trail of Tears: The **Removal Act of 1830** provided for resettlement of tribes to the West. The policy was implemented by Presidents Jackson and Van Buren.
- The remaining lands of the Five Civilized Tribes (the Cherokee had newspapers and a constitution) were ceded by treaty (with some compensation).
- The tribes were forced to make long treks (the Trail of Tears) to Indian Territory west of the Mississippi River.

Isolated resistance: Continued.
- In the Black Hawk War (1832) Illinois militia pursued and massacred tribespeople who had attempted to reoccupy lands.
- Seminoles fought a guerrilla war from the Florida Everglades until the early 1840s.

Key 45   Post-Jackson politics

OVERVIEW *Opposition to Jacksonian politics helped create a new political party (the Whigs), which captured the presidency in 1840 and 1848.*

Whig Party: Was a coalition of opponents of "Jacksonian tyranny."
- It attracted former National Republicans such as Daniel Webster and Henry Clay.
- The Anti-Masonic Party held the first national nominating convention in 1831. After receiving only 8% of the popular vote in 1832, most members joined the Whigs.
- Whigs supported a more active national government, economic development (Clay's American System), and humanitarian reform.

Democrats: In the Jefferson and Jackson traditions, distrusted concentrations of political and economic power.

Election of 1840: The first unified Whig candidacy.
- The number of eligible voters had greatly increased, and over 80% cast their ballots.
- Martin Van Buren was defeated for reelection by war hero **William Henry Harrison** ("Tippecanoe and Tyler Too!").
  1. The "log cabin and hard cider" campaign had popular appeal.
  2. Within a month Harrison was dead and John Tyler (more a Democrat than a Whig) succeeded to the office and *title* of president.

James K. Polk: The Democrat "dark horse" candidate in 1844 defeated Henry Clay (a third-time candidate).
- Polk accomplished the territorial expansion promised by his campaign (see Key 63).
- Domestic objectives such as tariff reduction and a reestablished independent treasury were also achieved in Polk's single term.

General Zachary Taylor: A war hero, he regained the White House for the Whigs in 1848.
- The Free Soil candidate drew votes from Taylor's opponent.
- On Taylor's death in 1850, **Millard Fillmore** became president.

Elections of 1852 and 1856: Won by Democrats **Franklin Pierce** and **James Buchanan**.
- Each was a Northerner with Southerner sympathies (*Doughface*).
- Weak executive leadership failed to deal effectively with growing sectional controversy.

Theme 8   AN ERA OF REFORM

A second cycle of evangelical religious "awakening" was a reaction to the rise of science and to rationalism. One result was the emergence of a number of new religious sects and denominations. In the pursuit of human perfection, a number of utopian communities were established, mostly in frontier areas. Humanitarian reform movements sought improvements in many fields: the condition of women, the existence of slavery, treatment of criminals, and the problem of alcoholism, among others. A romantic movement in the arts stressed American themes, self-reliant individualism, and an acknowledgment of the importance of emotional influences.

Key 46   The second Great Awakening

OVERVIEW   *A new cycle of emotional religious revivalism responded to the Age of Enlightenment and became the chief motivator for social reforms.*

Enlightenment: Put strains on Protestant Christianity.
- Deism, which rejected the Trinity, gained adherents during the Revolutionary Era, especially among intellectuals.
- Thomas Paine's *The Age of Reason* (1794) stressed rationalism and humanism.
- As Calvinism declined in New England, some turned to the New Unitarian or Universalist churches, which stressed God's oneness.

Transcendentalism: Some New England intellectuals, influenced by a new **Romantic** movement, followed a philosophy of **transcendentalism** (see Key 52).
- Partly as a result of Oriental religions' influence, mysticism reappeared.
- The stress on intuition elevated the importance of the individual.

Second Great Awakening: Beginning around 1800, it represented an emotional reaction to rationalism (emphasis on reason as the source of knowledge).
- Revivalist *camp meetings,* especially in the West, stirred participants' emotions.
- The fiery New York preacher Charles G. Finney became a promoter of social reform.
- Methodist Francis Asbury began sending *circuit riding* evangelists to remote Western areas.
- Baptist and Presbyterian denominations also flourished in the excitement of the Great Revival.
- Many denominations supported foreign missionary work.
- Women were often among the earliest and most enthusiastic converts.

New sects: Arose; some resulted from schisms (splits) of existing denominations.
- Most recognized the Bible as the sole source of authority and interpreted it literally.
- The Campbellites (later, Disciples of Christ) originated in western Pennsylvania.
- Adventists stressed the imminent Second Coming of Christ (later,

Seventh Day Adventists observed the Jewish Sabbath).
- Followers of William Miller (Millerites) in New England mathematically calculated the arrival of the millennium (a date in 1843, then 1844).
- The Burnt Over district of upper New York State was a particularly fertile producer of new faiths.
- Beginning with the Fox sisters (from rural Rochester area) spirit-rapping and seances (to communicate with the dead) enjoyed wide popularity.

Mormons: Church of Jesus Christ of Latter-Day Saints also originated in upstate New York.
- Joseph Smith experienced a series of miraculous visions.
- An angel directed him to golden tablets that, when translated, became known as the *Book of Mormon* (1830).
- Their cooperative communities were soon targets of local persecution.
- Mormon theocratic cohesion and charges of *polygamy* (multiple wives) fanned hostility.
- Smith was murdered by a mob in Illinois as the Mormons trekked westward.
- Brigham Young then led the exodus to the New Zion: the Great Salt Lake in Utah (1847).
- Efficient use of irrigation made possible a thriving and growing religious community.
- Admission of the Utah Territory to statehood was delayed until 1896 partly because of controversy over polygamy.

KEY FIGURE

Theodore Parker: A learned New England transcendentalist and preacher, he favored equality for women and abolition of slavery.

Key 47 Utopian communities

OVERVIEW *Religious, economic, and social experiments in communal living were recurrent in America, often reflecting dissatisfaction with changes that were occurring in society.*

The West: Religious freedom and plentiful cheap or free land attracted domestic and foreign religious communities.
- Cooperative societies provided an escape from the emerging competitive industrial and urban scene.
- Utopias created by religious groups began as early as the Mennonites at Ephrata, Pennsylvania in 1732.

Shakers: Began as a Quaker offshoot in England under Mother Ann Lee (the name derived from their ritual dance).
- By 1830 twenty communities existed in the United States.
- Self-sufficient agricultural settlements noted for their crafts began to wither due to the practice of celibacy.

Oneida community: John Humphrey Noyes led a Perfectionist religious community from Vermont to Oneida, New York.
- They met hostile reactions to the practice of *complex marriage* (free love).
- Successful small industry (including steel traps and silverware) enabled the community to survive to 1879.

Economic experiment: Robert Owen, a Scottish industrialist and humanitarian, founded a community at **New Harmony,** Indiana in 1825.
- Cooperative labor and collective ownership were to abolish poverty in his model town.
- Within two years the socialist experiment had succumbed to a fatal "disease of laziness."
- Other unsuccessful economic experiments were based on the socialist ideas of the Frenchman **Charles Fourier.**

Brook Farm: In Massachusetts; received great public attention because of the celebrities who were associated with it.
- Among the founders in 1841 were literary figures such as Ralph Waldo Emerson and Nathaniel Hawthorne.
- After five years of fair success, especially with their school, the community succumbed to debt.

Key 48 Reform movements

OVERVIEW *With a traditional belief in America's special mission, 19th century reformers sought to create a more perfect society.*

Sources: Religious awakening and belief in individual human perfectibility stimulated a variety of 19th century reform movements. Associations and societies seeking moral uplift multiplied rapidly. Reform was also stimulated by the political principles of Jacksonian democracy.

Temperance: This crusade aimed to combat the heavy consumption of alcohol in America.
- Religious leaders and employers supported the movement. Others were motivated by anti-immigrant bias.
- Alcoholism was seen as a cause of poverty and many social ills.
- The American Temperance Society was formed in Boston in 1826.
- Some favored moderation, others advocated total *prohibition* (total abstinence).
- By the 1850s over a dozen states, beginning with Maine, had adopted prohibition laws.

Health and diet: The focus of other reformers.
- Health and hygiene groups promoted better habits.
- Sylvester Graham (the cracker promoter) was a leading lecturer.

Crime and mental illness: Other reformers targeted **prisons** and **insane** asylums.
- New, more humane approaches to crime in Europe began to affect America.
- Criminal codes and punishments were eased.
- Imprisonment for debt became less common.
- Reports and petitions by **Dorothea Dix** helped improve institutions for the mentally ill, first in Massachusetts and then in other states.

Peace movements: Also followed Europe's lead after the Napoleonic Wars.
- American Peace Society was founded in 1828 under the leadership of **William Ladd,** a New England merchant.
- Support came from other reform groups, and particularly from women and from traditional pacifists such as Quakers.

Abolitionism: See Key 50.

Key 49   Women's rights

OVERVIEW *Women, who had been generally excluded from public life, began to form associations to promote their interests.*

Traditional gender role: Assigned to women was maintenance of the family and household.
- The *cult of domesticity* both idealized and restricted women.
- A double standard of morality prevailed (more restrictive of women than of men).
- Large families were common (though the birthrate was declining) and divorce was rare. Attempts at birth control increased, abortions were available to middle and upper class women (though outlawed in twenty states by 1860).
- Women received less education than men.
- Middle class women were able to do charitable work.
- Women were denied the vote and nearly all legal rights.

Reform movements: Women often met resistance when they joined or led reform movements. The anti-slavery movement split over the issue of female participation (1840).

Seneca Falls (N.Y.) Convention: Called by **Lucretia Mott** and **Elizabeth Cady Stanton** in 1848.
- It issued a Women's Declaration of Independence, a paraphrase of the 1776 document ("all men and *women* are created equal..."), which included a list of women's grievances.
- Women's movement leaders held subsequent annual conventions beginning in 1850.
- **Susan B. Anthony** became an outspoken advocate of women's rights.
- Some male reformers lent support, but many opposed the movement.

Successes: Limited gains and opportunities were achieved for some women by 1860.
- More women found employment in growing industry (see Key 56).
- Married women were granted control of property in twelve states.
- Some women promoted a movement for more comfortable clothing (so-called "Bloomer Costume").
- Some schools were opened to women, notably Troy Female Seminary (founded by Emma Willard in 1821), Oberlin College

(first coeducational college, 1837) and Mount Holyoke (first women's college, 1837).

- A few low paying professions were open to women, particularly nursing and elementary school teaching.
- Women made slower progress in higher education: Rebecca Mann Pennell was appointed first woman professor on equal standing with men (at Antioch College) in 1852.
- Some remarkable individuals broke through the barriers of prejudice. For example:
  1. Margaret Fuller was a leading Boston writer and critic.
  2. Elizabeth Blackwell received a medical degree in 1849 then set up a clinic for poor women and children.
  3. Sojourner Truth, a freed slave, was a leading abolitionist and activist for women's rights.
  4. Sarah and Angelina Grimke, from a prominent South Carolina slave-holding family, attacked slavery in speaking tours.

KEY QUOTATIONS

I desire you would remember the ladies and be more generous to them than your ancestors…all men would be tyrants if they could.

Abigail Adams,
letter to husband John, 1776

In education, in marriage, in religion, in everything, disappointment is the lot of women.

Lucy Stone, 1855

Key 50   Abolition

OVERVIEW *The moral crusade against slavery became the dominant reform movement by the 1830s with the growth of the abolitionist movement.*

Early anti-slavery movements: Objections to slavery before the American Revolution were not widespread.
* Resolutions and protests by Quakers and Mennonites occurred as early as the 17th century.
* Quaker John Woolman published an anti-slavery pamphlet (1754).
* The first anti-slavery society was established in 1775 in Philadelphia, where the first abolitionist convention was later held.
* A movement for **manumission** (freedom) developed in the Upper South. It stressed gradual, compensated emancipation and colonization abroad, but after a Virginia legislative debate (1832), the movement was silenced in the South.
* The **American Colonization Society** was formed in 1817. During Monroe's administration Congress appropriated money to found a colony (Liberia) on the west coast of Africa (1822). Few free blacks chose to voluntarily return to Africa.

Abolitionists:
* **William Lloyd Garrison** established *The Liberator*, an abolitionist newspaper, in 1831. He supported immediate liberation without compensation to owners.
* The American Anti-Slavery Society was founded in 1833. It later split over inclusion of women.
* **Wendell Phillips** in New England and **Theodore Weld** in the West were other leading abolitionists.
* Blacks played leading roles (see Key 62).

Opposition: Most viewed abolitionists as dangerous fanatics.
* A mob sacked the home of Lewis Tappan in New York.
* Elijah Lovejoy, abolitionist editor, was murdered by a mob in Alton, Illinois (1837).
* In 1836 the House of Representatives adopted a *Gag Rule* to block abolitionist petitions. It was repealed in 1844 through the efforts of former President John Quincy Adams.

Tactics: After the **Liberty Party**'s overwhelming defeat in 1840, abolitionists turned increasingly from moral suasion to militancy.

Key 51 Education

OVERVIEW *Human perfectibility, it was believed by reformers, could be greatly advanced through provision for educational opportunity.*

Educational opportunity: Was limited in the early 19th century.
- A predominantly rural, scattered population was a handicap.
- Many children were educated at home, in churches, or in private schools.

Public schools:
- New England took the lead in the movement for tax-supported public schools. **Horace Mann**, Secretary of the Massachusetts Board of Education, promoted education in his annual reports. (Mann said, "Education then, beyond all other devices of human origin, is a great equalizer of the conditions of men—the balance wheel of the social machinery.")
- **Thaddeus Stevens** successfully guided a state school law through the Pennsylvania legislature in 1834.
- North Carolina led the South in public education, but the South lagged behind the rest of the country in providing education.

Support: For public schools came from many sources.
- Political reformers wanted a literate, informed electorate.
- Workers wanted opportunity for their children.
- Industrial employers wanted a competent work force.
- Language and history courses could help Americanize immigrants and promote patriotism.
- Ethical behavior would be promoted through texts such as McGuffey's *Eclectic Readers*.
- Noah Webster's spellers and Jedediah Morse's geographies were other influential textbooks.

Colleges: Were still predominantly linked to religious denominations.
- Jefferson's University of Virginia (1819) provided both academic and "useful" knowledge.
- State universities emerged in the South and West.

Adult education: Opportunities to learn multiplied.
- A variety of institutes and societies existed, some endowed by wealthy philanthropists.
- The *lyceum* and Chautauqua movements provided popular public lectures.
- Subscription and, later, tax-supported public libraries were opened.

Key 52   An American culture

OVERVIEW *The "Age of the Common Man" saw the emergence of a distinctive American majority culture increasingly independent of, yet related to, European influences. A predominant* Anglo-American *culture had emerged by 1860. Minority cultures, notably African-American, survived underground.*

Romanticism: Represented a reaction to the Enlightenment in the arts (1770s to 1830s).
- Emphasis swung to the individual, the perfectible common man.
- Emotions and feelings were stressed over reason and science.

Transcendentalist writers: Stressed optimistic self-reliance.
- **Ralph Waldo Emerson**'s writings and lectures declared a kind of American intellectual independence with a stress on self-reliant individualism.
- **Henry David Thoreau**'s nonconformity was illustrated by his "experiment" in simple living (*Walden,* 1854).

American literature: Flowered in great variety.
- **Washington Irving** was the first widely acclaimed American author.
- Uniquely American themes were stressed by the novels of **Nathaniel Hawthorne** (*The Scarlet Letter*), **James Fenimore Cooper** (*Leatherstocking Tales*), **Herman Melville** (*Moby Dick*), and others.
- **Edgar Allan Poe** virtually invented horror and mystery stories.
- Poetry reached a wide audience. **Walt Whitman** ("I hear America singing...") stressed national themes.
- New England produced the first distinguished American historians (Bancroft, Parkman, Prescott).

Publications: Magazines, some illustrated, and newspapers began to reach a wide audience with the introduction of new printing machinery from Europe.
- The first penny daily was the New York *Sun* (1833).
- Horace Greeley's *New York Tribune* became the nation's most influential newspaper.

Music and theater: Gained popularity.
- European musical talent, such as Jenny Lind, the Swedish

Nightingale, toured the country, but native American themes also emerged (Stephen Foster's adaptations of American folk music).

- Overcoming religious resistance to theater, European touring groups drew growing audiences. America produced some noted actors (Edwin Forrest, Edwin Booth), but few notable plays.

American artists: Often went to Europe for training and patronage.

- Portraits of George Washington by Gilbert Stuart and Charles Willson Peale and battle scenes by John Trumbull idealized patriotic themes.
- Landscape painters glorified the spectacular natural environment (Hudson River school).

Architecture: Showed little originality.

- The Greek revival style in public buildings reflected both admiration for ancient Greek republics and for the contemporary Greek struggle for independence.
- Jefferson's home (Monticello) and the library of the University of Virginia were outstanding examples of the classical style.
- With Romanticism, a revival of the Gothic style in public and private buildings occurred.

KEY QUOTATION

Trust thyself: every heart vibrates to that iron string….Whoso would be a man, must be a non-conformist.

Ralph Waldo Emerson, "Self-Reliance" (1841)

Theme 9 NATIONAL GROWTH

*T*he decades before the Civil War witnessed dramatic national expansion. Population increased due to both domestic birthrate and immigration. While agriculture continued to be the economic backbone of the country, industry developed rapidly, particularly in textiles. The factory system created conditions that stimulated the labor union movement. Improvements in transportation and communication helped make possible rapid urban growth. The frontier continued to move westward, leaping the Great Plains to the Pacific. Along with this extraordinary growth, diversity and social disparities increased. The likelihood of conflict in the future was, therefore, enhanced.

Key 53   Opening the West

OVERVIEW *The movement of Americans westward was accelerated by the prospect of plentiful land as well as wealth from the fur trade and, later, valuable minerals.*

Migration westward: Increased following the American Revolution.
- Attempts to restrain settlement to east of the Appalachians had failed. (See Key 14.)
- Settlers from Virginia and the Carolinas moved into the *Watauga* colony (in western North Carolina) in the early 1770s.
- Led by Ethan Allen, Vermont secured independence from New York and became the fourteenth state in 1791.
- Daniel Boone and his men cut the Wilderness Road through the Cumberland Cap into Kentucky and Tennessee. Those states entered the Union in the 1790s.
- Fur trappers were usually the first whites to enter frontier areas.
- Generous federal land acts (1800 and 1804) encouraged farmers to migrate westward.
- Black slaves were brought west below the Ohio River.

Jeffersonian ideal: Envisioned a large agrarian democracy ("Empire for Liberty").
- The 1803 land acquisition opened vast new areas to settlement (see Key 34).
- Former Vice President Aaron Burr (after killing Hamilton in a duel in 1804) apparently was involved in a conspiracy to separate Louisiana and perhaps conquer Mexico. Burr was acquitted in a trial for treason (1807).
- Jefferson signed a bill in 1806 to build a National Road from Cumberland, Maryland, to western Virginia (it reached Illinois by 1818).

Frontier life: Was harsh and challenging.
- Dealing with the Indian inhabitants and clearing the land for farming posed physical challenges.
- Squatters often occupied land without legal claim.
- Little attention was paid to environmental damage.

California: Was settled most rapidly after gold was discovered in 1848.
- 49ers rushed for riches via Panama, by sea around Cape Horn, or overland.
- Rapid population brought statehood within two years (see Key 66).

Key 54 Agriculture

OVERVIEW *The family farm raising subsistence crops was gradually overshadowed by commercial agriculture made possible by technological changes.*

Agriculture: Remained the backbone of the American economy through the first half of the 19th century.
- The 1860 census showed over half of the population was still engaged in farming.
- By 1850 the *value* of manufactured goods, however, had come to exceed that of agriculture.
- Increased agricultural productivity made the growth of industry and urbanization possible.

Government land policies: Stimulated agricultural growth.
- The Land Act of 1796 set too high a price—even for some speculators.
- Subsequent acts reduced the minimum plot size and price per acre until, by 1820, eighty acres could be secured for $100.
- Preemption Acts in 1830 and 1841 gave some claim priorities to *squatters.*
- Western farmers continued to agitate for *free* land, finally achieved by the **Homestead Act** (1862).

Transportation: Improvements opened new markets for farm products.
- Canals and then railroads made concentration on staple commercial crops profitable.
- The Erie Canal opened upstate New York farm land and provided a gateway to the Great Lakes and the Midwest (see Key 57).

Technology: Helped revolutionize farming.
- McCormick's reaper (1834) was an early breakthrough.
- John Deere's steel plow was patented in 1837.
- Other machines made sowing, threshing, and baling easier.
- These machines were particularly useful on the large farms of the semi-arid Great Plains.

Changes in farming: Intensified as the Civil War approached.
- Grain and meat production shifted to the West.
- Northeastern farms supplied vegetables and dairy products to growing cities.
- Southern agriculture was increasingly dominated by King Cotton.
- Tenant farming and employment of hired hands increased.

Key 55   Industrial development

OVERVIEW *The Industrial "Revolution" moved from England to America after the American Revolution, thereby transforming the nation's economy.*

Colonial manufacturing: Had been centered in the household.
- Farmers, seeking self-sufficiency, devised their own machines.
- Household handicrafts (including spinning and weaving) were supplemented by independent village artisans.

England: Pioneered in textile technology and industrialization.
- Machinery was invented to save labor costs.
- Large, expensive machines were centrally located in factories.
- New sources of power (water and steam) added to industrial efficiency.
- Factories came to specialize in particular products.
- Mass markets could be reached by improvements in transportation.
- English laws unsuccessfully attempted to ban the export of machinery or the emigration of textile experts.

American textile industry: Began in New England.
- Capital was available from merchants whose commerce had suffered from Jefferson's Embargo and from the War of 1812.
- Postwar tariffs helped protect infant American industry (first protective tariff was passed in 1816).
- Swift-flowing New England rivers provided inexpensive water power.
- Population centers and improved transportation provided domestic markets (overseas sales later increased).
- Cotton textile industry was followed by a woolen industry and emergence of ready-made clothing.

Mass production: Systems gradually developed.
- **Eli Whitney** used machine tools to produce precise *interchangeable parts* for muskets (1798).
- Federal armories at Harper's Ferry and Springfield, Mass. stimulated the machine tool industry.
- Oliver Evans applied a steam engine to flour mill operation (1804).
- A process for mass producing clocks was devised in Connecticut.
- The *American System* of mass production came to be admired and copied abroad.

Inventions: Quickened the industrial pace.
- The Patent Act of 1790 provided financial incentives for inventors by legally protecting their devices (the Patent Office was established in 1802).
- New farm machinery helped revolutionize agriculture.
- Charles Goodyear received a patent for vulcanizing rubber (1844).
- Elias Howe's sewing machine (1846), later improved by Isaac Singer, was a temporary setback for the factory system, since it made home sewing easier.

Company organization: Was slowly revised.
- Most companies had been individually or family owned. Partnerships could recruit additional capital.
- Corporations, under state charters, could raise money from investors who would have limited liability. Earliest corporations involved banks and transportation companies.
- A group of investors formed the Boston Manufacturing Company in 1813.
- Managers were hired to supervise spinning and weaving processes under one roof.
- The Merrimack Company devised the Lowell System in 1822 (see Key 56).
- The Boston and New York Stock Exchanges were created to trade corporate shares.

Results of industrialization:
- Increased productivity began to feed mass consumer markets.
- Towns and cities grew around factories (see Key 58).
- Labor shortages stimulated immigration and encouraged inventiveness (see Key 59).
- Not all workers benefitted (see Key 56).
- The effects of boom-and-bust cycles were more broadly felt.
- Government was increasingly involved in promoting industry.

KEY FIGURE

Samuel Slater: Carried knowledge of English textile machinery and its operation with him when he emigrated in 1789. This enabled him to set up the first American cotton mill in Pawtucket, Rhode Island for Moses Brown, a Quaker capitalist.

Key 56   Labor movement

OVERVIEW   *Despite a chronic shortage of labor, conditions in the work place provoked early movements for labor unions.*

Textile mills: Located in New England, they sought a dependable labor supply (see Key 55).
  • The *Rhode Island System* employed families living in tenements in mill villages.
  • Employers exercised paternalistic control over workers' lives.
  • In Lowell, Massachusetts and other towns, young farm women were recruited for factory labor, many on a temporary basis.
  • These mill girls were housed in chaperoned dormitories.
  • The drive for company profits caused wages to be cut and hours lengthened (a 70-hour work week was typical).
  • Voluntary associations campaigned unsuccessfully for a 10-hour day.
  • Immigrant Irish women began to fill mill jobs in the 1840s.
  • Militancy declined as immigrant was pitted against "Yankee."

Urban settings: Generated more "outwork" where women tenement-dwellers were paid for piecework.

Union movement: As factory conditions worsened, craft associations turned increasingly political and militant.
  • *Wage slaves* (including children) often worked in unhealthy and unsafe environments.
  • Strikes (one of the earliest was at Paterson, New Jersey) were rare.
  • Working men's parties flourished briefly in some cities as Jacksonian democracy widened the vote. They then became a reform wing of the Democratic Party (the *Locofocos*).
  • Crafts unions formed a National Trades Union in Philadelphia in 1834.
  • Earlier unions had been charged with criminal conspiracy in the courts.
  • In *Commonwealth v. Hunt* (1842) the Massachusetts court ruled that forming a union was not illegal if their methods were "honorable and peaceful."
  • In 1840 the 10-hour day was established for federal government employees.
  • The Panics (depressions) of 1837 and 1857 were setbacks for the union movement, which remained weak and decentralized.

Key 57 Transportation and communication revolutions

OVERVIEW *Between 1815 and 1860, revolutionary changes in transportation and communication helped to transform the American economy, particularly in the North.*

Roads: Navigable waterways usually provided faster and cheaper transportation than trails or dirt roads.
- Planked (corduroy) roads and macadamized turnpikes began to be constructed. Privately funded, they profited by charging tolls.
- The **National Road**, from Cumberland, Maryland to Wheeling, Virginia was opened in 1818 (later extended to Illinois).
- Some members of Congress (Clay, Calhoun, J. Q. Adams) favored more federal funding for internal improvements but some questioned its constitutionality (see Key 37).

Steamboats: Began to compete with barges and flatboats in river transportation.
- Robert Livingston and Robert Fulton sent a steamboat *up* the Hudson River in 1807.
- Four years later the *New Orleans* traveled down the Ohio and Mississippi Rivers.
- Shallow-draft steamboats by the hundreds used the western rivers.
- Steam gradually replaced sail on the Atlantic (Cunard's trans-ocean route began in 1848).

Canal era: Initiated in New York State.
- The state legislature funded construction of a 363-mile engineering marvel connecting Albany on the Hudson with Buffalo on Lake Erie.
- Completed in 1825, the Erie Canal quickly became a profitable freight route and contributed to the rapid development of New York City.
- Many immigrants traveled West by way of the canal.
- Attempts by other states (Pennsylvania, Maryland) to duplicate New York's system were less successful.
- The Panic of 1837 cooled off canal fever.

Railroads: Construction began to boom in the 1830s.
- Steam locomotives were pioneered in England.
- John Stevens demonstrated a locomotive in New Jersey (1820).
- The Baltimore and Ohio Railroad opened 13 miles of track in

1830, carrying Peter Cooper's locomotive, the Tom Thumb.

- Iron rails and increased standardization of track gauge aided development.
- Cornelius Vanderbilt made a fortune, first in steamboats then with the New York Central Railroad.
- Congress began to provide railroad land grants (alternate sections along right of way).
- By 1840 there were over 3,000 miles of track; by 1860 ten times that mileage.

Communication: Underwent dramatic change.

- Just prior to the Civil War, the pony express enjoyed a brief but colorful success carrying mail.
- Samuel F. B. Morse demonstrated an experimental electric telegraph in 1844.
- By 1860, 50,000 miles of telegraph wires provided instantaneous communication over long distances.
- By the fall of 1861, telegrams could be transmitted coast to coast.
- Congress voted appropriations for a North Atlantic cable in 1857. It was completed in 1866.

Effects: Application of technology to improve transportation and communication systems helped to tie together the vast geographical expanse of the United States although sectional benefits were uneven.

- Expansion of the frontier was facilitated and agricultural production increased.
- Significant links were established between the industrial Northeast and the agricultural West. (With capital invested in land and slaves, less transportation development occurred in the South.)
- Specialization in industry and agriculture was encouraged.
- A national market was opened up and exports expanded.

Key 58   Urban growth

OVERVIEW *The rapid growth of urban population before the Civil War made the country more diverse and more complex.*

Growth of cities:
- Immigration from abroad and migration from rural areas helped push urban population (in towns of 8,000 and over) from 3.3% in 1790 to 16% by 1860.
- Rapid growth of industry and business caused cities to grow.
- Location at transportation centers (ports and inland road and rail centers) contributed to growth. New York City was first in population by 1830.
- Urban growth was most dramatic in the Northeast, and somewhat later in Midwestern centers such as Chicago and St. Louis.

City life:
- Separated work from the home more than was the case in rural areas.
- Improved transportation (railroads, horse-drawn street cars, etc.) enabled cities to expand.
- Immigrant ghettoes in port cities created a greater cultural diversity.
- Businesses and stores were able to enjoy greater specialization.
- Public entertainment and spectator sports developed.

Urban problems: Multiplied as services were unable to keep pace with growth.
- Overcrowded tenement buildings were unpleasant and unsafe.
- Impure water supplies and inadequate sewage disposal were threats to health. (Boston pioneered a piped sewage system in 1823, and New York City a piped water supply in 1842.)
- With street crime on the increase, cities began to organize police departments.
- Street children roamed urban centers engaging in petty crime.
- Tensions over employment and ethnic religious differences caused outbreaks of urban violence (see Key 59).
- The gap between wealth and poverty grew as both a middle class and an affluent elite class expanded in privileged urban neighborhoods.

Key 59 Immigration

OVERVIEW *The first wave of 19th century immigration to America brought millions of newcomers, primarily from Northern and Western Europe. Although enriching American society, the immigrants often faced opposition.*

Extensive migration in Europe: Including emigration to America, followed the Napoleonic Wars.
- Conditions in Europe provided a stimulus to leave.
- America offered abundant job opportunities and cheap land.
- Earlier arrivals sent back optimistic reports.
- Steamship lines advertised low trans-Atlantic fares.
- Immigrants faced a difficult voyage and were often victimized.
- Some, disenchanted after their arrival, returned to their homeland.
- Immigration as a percent of total population peaked between 1845 and 1855.

Irish: Came in largest numbers in the 1840s.
- Poverty and overcrowding as well as discontent with British rule provided motives.
- A potato blight brought famine and death to many tenant farmers in Ireland.
- Most settled in Eastern city ghettos in America.
- Many were employed as manual laborers (building railroads and the Erie Canal) or domestic servants.
- Irish voter groups became politically significant.
- Most Irish maintained a close identification with the Catholic Church.

Germans: Also arrived in large numbers.
- Economic depression and political conditions (failure of liberal reform in 1848) spurred emigration.
- To preserve their culture, many Germans settled in groups, often on Midwest farms.
- Many German immigrants who had had military training served in the Civil War.

Other groups: Scandinavians immigrated in considerable numbers (primarily for economic reasons) before the Civil War. The Swedes, Danes, and Norwegians were productive pioneer farmers in the Midwest.

- **Chinese** immigrants on the West Coast did much construction work, especially on railroads. They met with discrimination and their entry was barred completely by 1882.
- **Jews** in colonial times, were mostly "Sephardic" (of Spanish/Portugese origin). In the 19th century (before 1865) most came from Germany.

Discrimination: "Nativists" increasingly opposed immigrant groups that were not easily acculturated (absorbed). There were sometimes violent clashes.
- Irish Catholics were targeted by those who feared papal conspiracies.
- German Catholics also had a language handicap.
- Stereotypes aggravated public fears, including fear of threats to their jobs.
- A mob burned a Massachusetts convent in 1834.
- Political organizations resisting immigration climaxed in the formation of the American (Know-Nothing) Party in 1854 (see Key 68).
- Restrictive legislation failed to pass as the slavery crisis began to eclipse the anti-immigration movement.
- Over 2.5 million immigrants entered the United States in the 1850s, compared with 600,000 in the 1830s.

Theme 10 SLAVERY AND EXPANSION

*E*xpansion of cotton production in the South between 1800 and 1860 revived the importance of the slave labor system in that section. Social status was defined by ownership of slaves, with owners of large plantations representing a small but powerful elite class. The plight of blacks in slavery gave rise to resistance in a variety of forms. Growing numbers of free blacks played significant roles in the anti-slavery movement. The expansion of American territory that resulted from the war with Mexico reopened the controversy over the status of slavery in lands administered by Congress.

INDIVIDUAL KEYS IN THIS THEME

60 The slave system

61 The white South

62 Free blacks; anti-slavery

63 Manifest Destiny

64 The Texas problem

65 War with Mexico

Key 60   The slave system

OVERVIEW *Despite its contradiction of the Republic's democratic ideals, the slave-plantation system became firmly entrenched in the South, underscoring its sectional distinctiveness.*

Slavery: Was gradually abolished in the North after the Revolution and was fading in the South but then dramatically revived.
- Congress ended the foreign slave trade in 1808, but illegal smuggling continued.
- Eli Whitney's 1793 improvement of a cotton gin to separate the seed in upland cotton and development of the power loom produced new incentives for growing cotton.
- The value and price of slaves rose as tobacco, rice, and sugar plantations also employed gang labor.
- Cotton eventually represented over 50% of United States export values.
- As the Cotton Belt moved southwest to the Gulf States, the Upper South provided a domestic supply of slaves (Charleston and New Orleans were auction centers).

Slave system: Varied with the owner and type of work. Narratives by former slaves provide accounts of conditions.
- Larger plantations sought economic self-sufficiency.
- Slaves were treated as property and dehumanized, deprived of their African names, culture, religion.
- The owner's power over his slaves was virtually unlimited; women were frequently sexually exploited (reflected in large mulatto population).
- Cruelty and the discipline of the whip were common (but rarely to the point of disability).
- Slaves were provided with *limited* diet, clothing, housing (cabins), and medical care.
- Overseers (white) and drivers (usually black) supervised field workers (including women). House servants and artisans (on large plantations and in towns) enjoyed better conditions.
- Marriages were not recognized, but family and kinship cohesion were remarkable. The sale of slaves did not respect family ties.
- It was usually illegal to teach slaves to read or write.
- **Africanisms** survived as an African-American subculture in music, religion, and folklore (often with hidden meanings).

- Wealth, social class, and political power in the white South were determined to an increasing extent by the number of slaves owned.

Slave resistance: Took a variety of forms.
- Some played intentionally servile roles but slowed or sabotaged their work or feigned illness.
- Arson (a capital offense) or suicide were rarer occurrences.
- Flight (to a city, to the North, or Canada) was difficult since color defined status.
  1. Ohio Quaker **Levi Coffin** and others operated "underground railroads" to aid escapees.
  2. Runaway **Harriet Tubman** made frequent trips to the South to aid others. She also served as a spy and nurse in the Civil War.
- Slave insurrections, though rare, caused near panic among slave owners.
  1. The *Stono* Rebellion (1739) was an early South Carolina outbreak.
  2. *Gabriel*'s "conspiracy" (Richmond, 1800) was betrayed and suppressed.
  3. *Nat Turner*'s rebellion (Virginia, 1831) cost the lives of 60 whites and over 200 blacks. Turner and nineteen other conspirators were hanged.

National reactions: Slavery increasingly **divided** the nation.
- When the Supreme Court decided in 1842 that the fugitive slave law was constitutional but state officials did not have to enforce it, many Northern states passed *personal liberty laws.*
- The Methodist (1844) and Baptist (1845) churches split sectionally over slavery.
- Fear increased over a slave-power conspiracy to expand slavery in the territories.

KEY QUOTATION

Slaves sing when they are most unhappy....The songs of the slave represent the sorrows of his heart.

                                                             Frederick Douglass

Key 61   The white South

OVERVIEW *The slave labor system defined the Southern white social structure and was increasingly defended as essential to that section's way of life.*

Ownership of land and slaves: Defined social status in the South.
- The *planter* class (Bourbons) was small but had great social, economic, and political power.
  1. By 1860 only 0.5% owned 100 or more slaves.
  2. A paternalistic culture stressed a chivalric code of honor and deference to superiors.
  3. Wives were essential to the effective operation of the household and the plantation but adulation of women was contradicted by a double standard on sex.
  4. With population scattered, sons were frequently tutored or educated abroad.
- *Smaller plantations* were far more common. Almost half of owners held five or fewer slaves.
- *Yeoman* farmers owned *no* slaves and often produced corn and subsistence crops. Hill folk and poor whites could, however, consider themselves racially superior and hope to own slaves in the future.

Defense of slavery: While humanitarian reform was flourishing in the North, the South was skeptical of human perfectibility and defended the status quo.
- Biblical scripture was said to condone slavery. ("Servants obey your masters.")
- History showed great classical civilizations had been based on slavery.
- Africans, it was argued, were innately inferior. Pseudo-scientific evidence was offered for racial incapacity of blacks.
- Africans provided a necessary ("mud-sill") class of workers who were not affected by warm climate or diseases.
- Slaves were claimed to be better provided for and happier than the "wage slaves" of Northern factories.
- The slave system, it was argued, provided a controlled and orderly society less prone to social and political radicalism than the factory system of the North.
- Senator **John C. Calhoun** of South Carolina argued in 1837 that slavery was "instead of an evil, a good—*a positive good.*"
- As disputes over slavery's expansion grew, the defense of the institution in the South hardened.

Key 62   Free blacks; anti-slavery

OVERVIEW   *The growing number of freed blacks played a crucial role in the agitation for emancipation before the Civil War.*

Free blacks: Numbered 60,000 in 1790 and 500,000 (11% of the black population) by 1860. Over half lived in the South; many were mulattoes (mixed-race).
- Freedom was achieved by state laws, freeing by private owners, by fleeing, by military service, or by self-purchase.
- Free blacks were domestics, artisans, laborers, sailors.

Restrictions: Freedom was **limited** by prejudice and laws.
- **Black Codes** in the South restricted activity. Freedom-papers had to be carried, and civil and political rights were often denied.
- In the North, restrictions were less severe, but white supremacy also prevailed. White immigrants were often rivals for jobs.
- Racial violence sometimes broke out, especially in cities.

Black associations: Were formed for mutual help.
- African Methodist and Baptist churches were of central importance to communities.
- Self-help societies and fraternal groups were founded.
- Black national conventions in the 1830s and '40s attacked slavery and argued for equal rights, as did militant black newspapers.
- Eight states sent delegates to the 1853 convention in Rochester, New York where the *Declaration of Sentiments* supported manual training schools but rejected emigration from the country.

Black individuals: Provided inspiration.
- In the 1790s **Benjamin Banneker**'s achievements as a mathematician and astronomer were judged "exceptional" by Thomas Jefferson.
- **Phillis Wheatley**, brought from Africa as a slave at age eight, had a volume of poetry published in 1773.
- **David Walker**'s *Appeal* (1830) urged slaves to fight for their freedom.
- **Henry Garnet**, a fiery abolitionist, urged armed rebellion, if necessary. ("Rather die free men than live to be slaves")
- **Frederick Douglass**, a self-taught runaway, became a great orator, the editor of *The North Star*, a supporter of feminism, and, in 1889, was appointed United States Minister to Haiti.

Key 63   Manifest Destiny

OVERVIEW *Agitation and actions to expand United States territory to continental limits gave rise to political and sectional controversies.*

Canada: Canadian-American relations had been improved by 1817 and 1818 treaties (see Key 39).
- When some Americans lent sympathetic support to a rebellion in Canada in 1837, a small American vessel was destroyed by Canadian loyalists.
- Britain's refusal to return mutinous slaves who had seized the U.S. merchant ship *Creole* and a minor conflict on the sparsely populated Maine border caused some clamor for seizure of Canadian territory.
- The Webster-Ashburton Treaty (1842) provided for joint U.S.-British patrols to suppress the African slave trade and settled the Canadian border dispute.

Oregon: Had been jointly occupied by Britain and the United States since 1818.
- John Jacob Astor's American Fur Company had set up trading stations in the Columbia River area before the War of 1812.
- Methodist missionaries and settlers entered the Willamette Valley in the 1830s.
- Sizeable migrations entered over the Oregon Trail in the 1840s.
- During Polk's presidential campaign of 1844, the expansionist slogan "54°40' or fight!" was used.
- With expansion pending in the Southwest (see Key 64), the United States agreed to accept the extended 49th parallel in an 1846 treaty with Britain.

The Pacific: United States interests there were expanding.
- Whaling ships and missionaries arrived in the Hawaiian Islands in the 1830s.
- An annexation treaty with the Hawaiian government in 1854 was dropped after foreign and domestic protests.
- Swift-sailing clipper ships established a small but profitable trade with East Asia.
- After the Opium Wars, diplomat Caleb Cushing negotiated the Treaty of Wanghia (1844), which secured U.S. trading rights in some Chinese ports.
- The Fillmore administration dispatched Commodore Matthew

Perry and his "black ships" to the reclusive Japanese islands in 1853. The shogun bowed to the threat of superior American technology.
- Five years later Townsend Harris secured a trade treaty with Japan, helping to propel that country toward Westernization.

The Caribbean: Another target for Manifest Destiny (Southern extremists welcomed the prospect of new slave territory).
- Spain rejected a U.S. offer to buy Cuba in 1848.
- Private filibusterers (soldiers of fortune) attempted to seize Cuba (1848) and Nicaragua (William Walker in 1855–60).
- When Spain again rejected an offer to buy Cuba, American diplomats in Europe issued the Ostend Manifesto, threatening to seize the island.

Gadsden Purchase (1853): A slice of land bought from Mexico for possible railroad construction completed acquisition of contiguous (adjacent) territory on the continent.

Alaska: Purchased from Russia in 1867 for $7,200,000.
- President Andrew Johnson's Secretary of State, William Seward, was an ardent expansionist.
- Despite misgivings about the "worthless icebox" of Seward's Folly the Senate approved the acquisition treaty.

KEY QUOTATION

Our manifest destiny is to overspread the continent allotted by Providence for the free development of our yearly multiplying millions.
Editor John Louis O'Sullivan, 1845

Key 64   The Texas problem

OVERVIEW *Americans who had settled in northern Mexico first achieved independence from Mexico and then sought annexation to the United States.*

Claims to Texas: Had been given up when the U.S. signed the Florida treaty with Spain (1819), defining the borders of the Louisiana territory (see Key 39).
- Mexican independence from Spain (1821) was followed by civil turmoil.
- Twice Mexico rejected offers by the U.S. to purchase Texas, part of its northernmost state.

American settlers: Were lured to Texas with offers of large tracts of free land.
- **Stephen F. Austin** and others led groups of American immigrants into Texas.
- Under the 1825 Colonization law, settlers were expected to become Roman Catholics and Mexican citizens.
- Some brought slaves although slavery was banned by Mexico after 1830.
- When Mexico tried to close its borders, illegal American immigrants continued to enter.

Rebellion: After General Santa Anna seized power in Mexico and attempted to centralize control, rebellious Texans declared their right to secede.
- Independence was declared (March 1836) and a constitution drawn up.
- Santa Anna wiped out the Texan defenders at the Alamo at San Antonio.
- **Sam Houston**'s forces defeated the Mexicans at San Jacinto, capturing Santa Anna.
- Texan independence was recognized by the United States Congress (July 1836).

The Lone Star Republic (1836–45): Elected Sam Houston president, and requested annexation to the U.S.
- Texan request for annexation was opposed by those Americans who feared expansion of slave territory and the petition was refused.

- During nine years of independence the Republic of Texas inched toward annexation.
- Britain and France extended recognition and trade to Texas.

Annexation treaty: Failed to get the necessary two-thirds Senate approval but was approved by joint resolution (a simple majority vote) just before Polk's inauguration (March 1845).
- Mexico broke diplomatic relations with the U.S.
- John Slidell's mission to negotiate a settlement (including purchase of California) failed (March 1846).

War begins: American troops, under General Zachary Taylor, sent into disputed territory between the Rio Grande and Nueces Rivers, were attacked by Mexican forces.
- In his War Message (May 11, 1846), President Polk claimed Mexico was the aggressor.
- Congress voted overwhelmingly for war (40–2 in the Senate; 174–14 in the House. All opposition votes were from the North).
- However, opposition to the war began to grow almost immediately, particularly in the North, among anti-slavery groups.

KEY QUOTATION

[Mexico] has passed the boundary of the United States, has invaded our territory, and shed American blood upon the American soil.

Polk, War Message

Key 65   War with Mexico

OVERVIEW *War with Mexico resulted in the acquisition of nearly half of that nation's land and the reopening of the slavery controversy in American territories.*

Mexico: Appeared to have advantages: fighting on its own soil, with a larger and more experienced army, and with the hope of foreign aid.

American victories: General Zachary Taylor's army won victories at Monterrey and at Buena Vista, occupying much of Northern Mexico.
- An American fleet blockaded the Gulf Coast.
- General Winfield Scott's army made an amphibious landing near Veracruz, taking the city after a siege. Many of Scott's troops died of disease.
- The Americans then marched to Mexico City and took the capital.

California: An exploratory expedition under John C. Fremont entered California and endorsed the rebel Bear Flag Republic (June 1846). Colonel Stephen Kearney invaded New Mexico and then joined Fremont in California.

Opposition to the war: Led by Northerners who opposed the spread of slavery.
- Whig Congressman Abraham Lincoln's Spot Resolution challenged Polk's account of the war's origins.
- Henry David Thoreau's essay, "Civil Disobedience," called for nonviolent opposition to an evil war to expand slavery.
- An attempt (the Wilmot Proviso) to ban slavery from any territory acquired from Mexico repeatedly failed to pass the Senate.

Treaty of Guadalupe Hidalgo (1848): The U.S. secured California, the New Mexico Territory, and recognition of the Rio Grande as the Texas border.

Effects of the war:
- American territory was increased by a third. Its continental territory now reached to the Pacific Ocean.
- Additional Native Americans and Latinos were added to the population.
- Mexico received a payment of $15 million, but Mexican resentment was long-lasting. (Spanish cultural addition was significant.)
- The question of slavery in the territories was reopened.
- The war contributed to disunity within both the Whig and Democratic Parties, particularly over the slave territory question.

Theme 11 CONFLICT APPROACHES

*T*he American tradition of compromise again appeared to solve the troublesome question of slavery in the western territories. As the generation's great orators and compromisers passed from the scene, however, the emotional controversy began to heat up. Popular sovereignty reopened the opportunity for the expansion of slavery and led to civil conflict in Kansas. The slavery controversy splintered political parties and was intensified by a series of provocative events, including a controversial Supreme Court decision. The election of Republican Abraham Lincoln in 1860 caused South Carolina to secede from the Union. Last minute compromise efforts before Lincoln's inauguration failed.

INDIVIDUAL KEYS IN THIS THEME

Key 66 Compromise of 1850

OVERVIEW *Following the War with Mexico, Congress attempted to settle the slave controversy through compromise. The inclusion of a new fugitive slave act, however, gave rise to new antagonisms.*

California: Applied for admission to the Union following the Mexican War and the gold rush population increase. Admission as a free state would upset the balance of free and slave states in the Senate.

Debate: In the Senate's Golden Age, great orators debated.
- The dying John C. Calhoun proposed a theory of a *concurrent majority* (see Key 43).
- Daniel Webster of New England spoke for conciliation (7th of March Speech).
- Henry Clay (the Great Compromiser) proposed an 8-part Omnibus Bill to settle the controversy.

Compromise of 1850: Was actually five separate bills. Once again a sectional clash appeared to have been averted through compromise.
- California would enter the Union as a free state.
- New Mexico territory was created, and the Texas border was set.
- Utah territory was created. In both new territories *popular sovereignty* would decide the slave question.
- The slave *trade* was abolished in the District of Columbia.
- A new, stronger, Fugitive Slave Law was enacted.
  1. Fee arrangements encouraged commissioners to certify *runaways* (although some were free blacks).
  2. No jury trials were permitted.

Reaction: Resistance to the new Fugitive Slave Law grew in the North.
- Some states passed "personal liberty laws" to inhibit enforcement.
- The underground railroad increased activity (see Key 62).
- In a few cases mobs resisted the return of alleged runaways.
- The Supreme Court in *Ableman v. Booth* (1859) unanimously reaffirmed the constitutionality of the Fugitive Slave Law.

Key 67 Kansas-Nebraska

OVERVIEW *A bill to organize two new western territories reopened the slavery controversy and resulted in a prelude to civil war.*

Transcontinental railroad: Projects were proposed in the 1850s to follow several possible routes (see Key 63).
- The chosen route would economically benefit the section through which it would pass.
- Northern boosters favored several possible routes.

Kansas-Nebraska Bill: Introduced by Senator **Stephen Douglas** of Illinois in 1854.
- Two territories, Kansas and Nebraska, would be formed (facilitating a central railroad route from Chicago).
- Slavery in those territories would be determined by popular sovereignty (majority vote).
- The 36°30' line established by the Missouri Compromise was now erased (see Key 38).
- Despite enraged responses President Pierce signed the bill into law (see Key 68).

Bleeding Kansas: Northern free soilers and abolitionists and pro-slavery settlers from neighboring Missouri flooded into Kansas.
- In a disputed election, pro-slavery forces won control of the territorial legislature, which enacted a severe slave code.
- Free soilers, in a clear majority, drew up a rival Topeka Constitution, which provided for ending slavery.
- Supporters of the rival governments fought pitched battles.
- Abolitionist **John Brown** led a vicious attack on a settlement at Pottawatomie Creek.
- Guerrilla warfare necessitated the calling of federal troops.

Popular sovereignty: The 1857 Dred Scott decision (see Key 70) raised a question regarding popular sovereignty: Could a territorial government ban slavery when it applied for statehood?
- Topeka (free) and Lecompton (slave) governments both petitioned Congress for Kansas statehood.
- President Buchanan backed the pro-slavery constitution.
- With Senator Douglas's support, a Kansas revote overwhelmingly rejected the Lecompton constitution.
- Admission of Kansas as a free state was delayed until 1861.

Key 68   Political party changes

OVERVIEW *Controversies over slavery in the territories contributed to the splintering of old political parties and the emergence of new parties.*

Anti-slavery factions: Angered by the tactics employed by defenders of slavery (see Key 62), turned to politics.
- The *Liberty Party*'s abolitionist candidate for president in 1844, James G. Birney, won just over 2% of the popular vote but affected the outcome of the election by drawing votes from the Whigs, particularly in New York.
- A new *Free Soil Party* (not abolitionist but opposed to territorial expansion of slavery) in 1848 won 10% of the popular vote with former president Martin Van Buren as their candidate. Again, drawing votes away aided the election of Taylor.
- The Free Soil vote fell 50% in 1852 when their candidate repudiated the 1850 Compromise.

Whig Party: Split over the slavery issue.
- Southern, "Cotton" Whigs drifted into the Democratic Party.
- Northern, "Conscience" Whigs moved to new parties (Free Soil and, later, Republican).

American Party ("Know-Nothings"): A nativist third party that relied upon "xenophobia" (fear of foreigners) and on the temperance movement (see Key 59).
- In 1856 former president Millard Fillmore, the Know-Nothing candidate, won over 21% of the popular vote and Maryland's 8 electoral votes.
- The American Party was absorbed by the Republicans after 1856.

Republican Party: Formed as a coalition in 1854.
- At Ripon, Wisconsin and Jackson, Michigan, Independent Democrats, Free Soilers, and Conscience Whigs united in opposition to the Kansas-Nebraska bill.
- This third party stressed free labor and opposed the *extension* of slavery in the territories ("Free Soil, Free Labor, Free Men!").
- In Illinois, Abraham Lincoln returned to politics as a Whig but cooperated with Republicans.
- John C. Fremont, a military hero, was the first Republican presidential candidate in 1856.
- To maintain unity, the Democrats nominated **James Buchanan**, who won the 1856 election partly by sweeping the South.

Key 69   Friction and violence

OVERVIEW *As Northern opposition to the expansion of slavery grew, willingness to compromise declined and incidents of emotional incitement to violence increased.*

Uncle Tom's Cabin: The 1852 novel by **Harriet Beecher Stowe** dramatized slave conditions.
* Based on limited factual observation but fired by anger over the new Fugitive Slave Law, Stowe's book was melodramatic and filled with stereotypes.
* It was a success both as a book and as a stage drama.
* It heightened emotional tension in the North and the South.

The Impending Crisis of the South: By Hinton Helper of North Carolina, published in 1857.
* It attempted to prove that non-slave-holding poor whites were hurt most by slavery.
* Published in the North, it stirred emotions in both sections.

Violence in the Senate: Senator Charles Sumner (Massachusetts) in 1856 delivered a fiery anti-slavery speech, including condemnation of Senator Andrew Butler (South Carolina). Butler's nephew, Congressman Preston ("Bully") Brooks, beat Sumner with a cane at his Senate desk.

Harper's Ferry: John Brown (see Key 67) performed the most incendiary deed in 1859.
* With a small following he occupied the federal arsenal at Harper's Ferry, Virginia, hoping to set off a slave rebellion.
* He had the financial backing of prominent abolitionists (the Secret Six).
* Brown was wounded, taken prisoner, quickly tried for treason against the state, and hanged at Charlestown (December 2, 1859).
* Rumors of insurrection terrified the South.

KEY FIGURE

John Brown: A religious fanatic and abolitionist crusader, he led attacks on slave-holders in Kansas. After he was captured at Harper's Ferry, tried, and executed, he was branded a dangerous madman by many in the South but hailed as a martyr by many in the North.

Key 70   Dred Scott decision

OVERVIEW *The focus of the slavery controversy shifted dramatically from Congress to the Supreme Court with the Dred Scott decision. That decision and the doctrine of popular sovereignty were debated by Lincoln and Douglas.*

The Supreme Court: With a pro-South majority, it became a bulwark for the defense of slavery.

Dred Scott: This *test case* was promoted by anti-slavery groups.
- Scott's owner, an army surgeon, had taken him to posts in a free state and in free territory.
- His suit for freedom passed through the Missouri (slave state) courts.
- Since his new owner lived in New York, the case could be appealed to the federal courts.
- The U.S. Supreme Court heard the case in 1856 but delayed decision because of the presidential election. (Buchanan was aware of the outcome; suspicions of a "slave power conspiracy" were revived.)

Decision: Chief Justice Taney's 1857 decision spoke for a 6–3 majority (though others wrote opinions). Two Northern Republicans wrote strong dissents. Taney wrote:
- Scott was not a citizen and had no standing in court. (Taney's racism was revealed when he referred to Negroes as "an inferior order.")
- Scott's residence in a free state and territory had not made him free since he returned to Missouri.
- Congress had no right to prohibit slavery in a territory. This voided an act of Congress (Missouri Compromise) for only the second time (see Key 32).

Reaction: By the public and in Congress was heated.
- In **Illinois** Abraham Lincoln and incumbent Senator Stephen Douglas campaigned for the Senate with a series of debates in 1858.
- Lincoln tried to focus on the Dred Scott decision's impact on popular sovereignty (see Key 67).
- In the Freeport Doctrine, Douglas responded that anti-slavery territories could refuse to enact slave codes.

Key 71 Election of 1860; secession

OVERVIEW *With the Democratic party divided, the election of a Republican president who opposed the extension of slavery caused the first Southern states to secede from the Union.*

Panic of 1857: Temporarily distracted attention from the slavery controversy.
  * Overspeculation in land and railroads and international conditions were among the complicated causes.
  * The Northeast was hardest hit by the resultant two-year depression (further intensifying sectionalism).
  * Eastern workers and Western farmers were attracted to the new Republican party.

1858 Congressional elections: Resulted in Republican gains, as the Democrats were hurt by disputes between President Buchanan and Senator Douglas (for Lincoln-Douglas Senate contest see Key 70).

Democratic Party: Finally split at its 1860 convention in Charleston, South Carolina.
  * When a proposed platform defending slavery was defeated, Deep South delegates walked out.
  * Reassembling in Baltimore in June, the convention nominated **Stephen Douglas** for president with a platform opposing Congressional interference with slavery.
  * The Southerners then met and nominated **John Breckenridge** of Kentucky with a pro-slavery platform.

Republican Party: Met in Chicago, Illinois.
  * Local supporters in the galleries helped **Abraham Lincoln** secure the nomination on the third ballot.
  * The platform opposed the extension of slavery but defended the right of states to control their own "domestic institutions."
  * Broad support was gained through planks favoring a homestead act, a protective tariff, and transportation improvements.

Constitutional Union Party: A convention dominated by moderates from border states, nominated **John Bell** of Tennessee with a reconciliation platform.

Election of 1860: Lincoln won with a plurality (just under 40%) of the popular vote but an electoral majority in the four-man race.

Secession: An *Ordinance of Secession* was adopted by a South Carolina convention on December 20, 1860.
- In their declaration of causes, they blamed the election of a sectional president "hostile to slavery."
- Six other Deep South states, led by extremists, left the Union by the following February.
- Texas secession came through a referendum after Governor Sam Houston had opposed separation.
- Four Upper South states (Virginia, Tennessee, Arkansas, and North Carolina) rejected secession until after Lincoln's inauguration and the firing on Fort Sumter. Each of these states had significant pockets of pro-Union sympathy.

President Buchanan: A *lameduck,* and a "doughface" (Northerner with Southern sympathies) he refused to "coerce" the states even when secessionists began to seize federal property.

Compromise efforts: however hopeless, continued.
- Senator John Crittenden (Kentucky) proposed amendments protecting slavery where it existed and in territories south of 36°30'.
- A February (1861) Peace Conference in Washington presided over by ex-president Tyler also failed.
- Thomas Corwin (Ohio) proposed an amendment guaranteeing slavery where it existed. It was adopted by Congress on inauguration day but was, of course, never ratified.

Theme 12 CIVIL WAR

*A*fter the Southern states seceded, the federal government sought to hold its forts on Southern soil and to keep border states from joining the Confederacy. The Union appeared to have formidable advantages at the outset of the fighting. The Confederate government needed to mobilize a unified effort contrary to its states rights philosophy. The four-year military struggle brought drastic changes on the home fronts, including greatly increased power for the central government. The Union's naval blockade and success at minimizing foreign aid to the South were important factors in the outcome. The war to preserve the Union had also become the war to end slavery.

INDIVIDUAL KEYS IN THIS THEME

Key 72 Civil War begins

OVERVIEW *The new Lincoln administration faced the problems of suppressing secession, of retaining the border states, and of protecting federal property in the South.*

Inauguration: By Lincoln's Inauguration, seven Southern states had already seceded from the Union.
- On the long train ride from Springfield the president-elect was hurried in disguise through Baltimore because of fears of assassination.
- In his First Inaugural Lincoln emphasized that the Union was "perpetual."
    1. He promised not to interfere with slavery "in the States where it exists."
    2. He denied secession's legality.
    3. He vowed to preserve the Union in the face of "insurrection."

Border slave states: Were a matter of concern to the Lincoln government.
- Delaware had few slaves, but Maryland's secession could have surrounded Washington. Lincoln's imposition of martial law (see Key 78) and a pro-Union election result secured that key state.
- Missouri was bitterly divided and became a battleground, particularly on the Arkansas border.
- Kentucky attempted neutrality (it was both Lincoln's and Davis's state of birth), but Confederate armed intervention led to Union countermeasures.

Difficult choices of loyalty: Faced many (Robert E. Lee, for example) and literally divided some families.

Fighting begins: Forts in the South at Pensacola, Florida and at Charleston, South Carolina (Fort Sumter) were still in federal hands. Lincoln dispatched a relief ship with supplies for Sumter.
- On Confederate government orders, General Beauregard delivered an ultimatum and then opened fire on Sumter, which surrendered in 36 hours.
- The next day Lincoln called for 75,000 militia (for 3 months) to suppress the rebellion and then proclaimed a blockade of rebel ports in the South.

The North: Appeared to have significant advantages at the beginning of the War:

- The North had a population advantage of 22 million to 9 million (and over 3 to 1 of white males of military age).
- Over 90% of the nation's manufacturing (including nearly all heavy industry) was located in the North.
- The North (and West) had diverse agriculture, which it was able to greatly expand.
- The North had a great edge in capital wealth (even if the South's slaves were included).
- Transportation systems (notably railroads) were far superior.
- The North had nearly all the civilian shipping and most of the navy.
- A more nationalistic, centralized government structure was already in place. (Lincoln turned out to be a notably effective wartime leader.)

The South: Apparent advantages included:
- Slaves ($1/3$ of the population) freed more whites to fight.
- A vast geographic area, familiar to its defenders, would presumably have to be invaded and conquered by the North.
- Cotton exports could pressure textile-manufacturing Britain to provide aid.
- The South had a strong military tradition.
- Many veteran military leaders (including Lee) remained loyal to the South (officers on both sides had served together in the Mexican War).
- The South was hampered by its commitment to states rights and localism ("excessive democracy?").

KEY QUOTATION

In *your* hands, my dissatisfied fellow-countrymen, and not in *mine*, is the momentous issue of civil war....You can have no conflict without being yourselves the aggressors.

Abraham Lincoln, First Inaugural Address

Key 73   The Confederacy

OVERVIEW *To accomplish its "conservative revolution," the South needed to create a new government while pursuing the war effort.*

Confederate States of America: A government was formed at Montgomery, Alabama, in February 1861.
- Support for secession was strongest where slaveholding was most prevalent. (Yet 44% voted against secession in Alabama; and there were numerous pro-Union areas through the South.)
- **Jefferson Davis** (Mississippi) was elected president (for a single, six-year term) and Alexander Stephens (Georgia) vice president.
- Delegates adopted a constitution, duplicating the U.S. Constitution in many respects, but with state sovereignty acknowledged. Slavery and transporting of slaves were protected; the president was given an "item veto"; protective tariffs were banned.
- After Lincoln's inauguration, Virginia and three other states joined the Confederacy; the capital was moved to Richmond in June.

Problems: Political bickering hampered the South.
- Each state was represented in a cabinet whose membership frequently changed.
- Competing political parties never emerged.
- The centralization of power necessary to conduct war conflicted with commitment to states rights. (Georgia objected to "military dictatorship," for example).

Conscription Act (April 1862): Drafted white men aged 18 to 35 for three years.
- Substitutes could be bought and many inequities existed.
- Large slave-holders were exempted, causing class resentment.
- Desertions became a major problem as the war progressed.
- Slaves were used as laborers but were not armed until the war's end.

Financing the war:
- Taxes were inequitable and inadequate and were resisted; funds were raised by printing national and state bonds and paper currency.
- Resultant inflation reached over 9,000% in four years (compared with 117% in the North).
- Refugees contributed to a growing food crisis, and in 1863 women led bread riots in several Southern cities.
- Despite some success with blockade-running, there were shortages of everything.

Key 74   Bull Run to Chancellorsville (1861–63)

OVERVIEW *Early enthusiasm by both sides over the prospect of a short war was quickly shattered. Over 600,000 (2% of the population) died in four years of fighting.*

Union strategy: Stressed a naval blockade, gaining control of the Mississippi River, and military campaigns in eastern Tennessee and against Richmond (the two capitals were only 100 miles apart).

Bull Run (Manassas, Virginia): The scene of the war's initial major battle (July 21, 1861).
- Jackson stood like a "stone wall" as Confederate reinforcements arrived by railroad (illustrating technology's impact).
- After the confused clash, Union soldiers (and civilian spectators) fled to Washington in panic.
- Lincoln called for 100,000 troops for three years and appointed George McClellan general-in-chief.

McClellan: Excelled at organizing troops and stirring enthusiasm.
- Though fearful of risks, he was pressured to launch the *Peninsula Campaign.*
- Slowly approaching Richmond, the Union Army of the Potomac won 4 of 5 battles and then retreated (McClellan was relieved by Lincoln).

Robert E. Lee: Commander of Confederate Army of Northern Virginia.

Shenandoah Valley (Virginia): Attacks by Jackson's Confederates diverted attention from Richmond; General John Pope was replaced by McClellan after losing second battle of Bull Run to Lee.

The West: General Ulysses S. Grant drove the Confederates from Kentucky then won key victories over Johnston at Forts *Henry* and *Donelson* in western Tennessee. At *Shiloh* (Tennessee) both sides suffered heavy casualties.

Antietam: Lee invaded Maryland (September 1862), where the Battle of *Antietam* (Sharpsburg) proved to be the war's bloodiest day.
- McClellan failed to pursue Lee, but Lincoln followed the "victory" with the Emancipation Proclamation (see Key 79).

Union defeats: *Fredericksburg,* Virginia (December) was a serious Union defeat, and at *Chancellorsville* in May, Lee maneuvered brilliantly but lost his able "right arm": Stonewall Jackson.

Key 75   Gettysburg to Appomattox (1863–65)

OVERVIEW   *The third year of the war began with two key Union victories, followed by Sherman dividing the Confederacy and the final siege of Richmond.*

Gettysburg (July 1–3, 1863): After Chancellorsville, Lee decided to invade the North again.
- Hoping to take Harrisburg and attack Washington from the north, Lee clashed by accident with the Army of the Potomac at Gettysburg, Pennsylvania.
- Pickett's charge again illustrated the new defensive advantage (new bullets in breech-loaded rifles, for example). (See Key 80).
- Meade failed to follow up as the Army of Northern Virginia retreated south in the rain.

Vicksburg: In Mississippi; fell the next day (July 4).
- Grant had outflanked the key city and besieged it for six weeks.
- The Mississippi River was now in Union control, cutting off Confederate supplies from the west.

War west of the Mississippi: Confederates and Unionists clashed in scattered small campaigns.
- Texas troops were defeated in New Mexico (Glorieta Pass).
- Sioux Indian uprising in Minnesota escalated to a general plains war in the Dakotas.

Tennessee: Union troops were besieged at Chattanooga.
- A series of Union victories (November 1863) provided the base for William T. Sherman's offensive.
- Lincoln had at last found an aggressive general in Grant, who was called to the East.

Georgia: Invaded by Sherman's Army, using *total war* tactics.
- Civilian support was undermined by systematic physical destruction.
- Atlanta fell after a month-long siege (September 1864), and Sherman then reached the sea at Savannah (December 21).
- Living off the land, the Union army marched north, taking South Carolina's capital and invading North Carolina by the war's end.

Virginia: Grant, now general-in-chief, pursued Lee's army south through Virginia's "Wilderness."
- Petersburg (south of Richmond) was reached after a series of battles.
- Lee's outnumbered forces endured ten months of trench warfare before abandoning Petersburg.
- Meanwhile, Sheridan's Union cavalry was devastating the Shenandoah Valley, Lee's "breadbasket."

End of the war: Richmond was evacuated April 2. Lincoln visited the city and was acclaimed by freed blacks.
- Lee's trapped and depleted army surrendered at Appomattox Court House on April 9.
- Jefferson Davis was captured in Georgia a month later and imprisoned.
- All other Confederate forces had surrendered by the end of May.

The assassination of President Lincoln: Occurred at Ford's Theatre five days after Appomattox.
- John Wilkes Booth, the assassin, was shot while fleeing through Virginia.
- Four "conspirators" were quickly tried by a military commission and hanged in July.

KEY FIGURES

Robert E. Lee: After declining Lincoln's offer of command of the U.S. Army, he brilliantly led the Confederate Army of Northern Virginia. After the war he became president of Washington College, Virginia, now called Washington and Lee.

Ulysses S. Grant: Famed for his insistence on unconditional surrender at Ft. Donelson, he forcefully applied the advantages of the North's manpower and material, yet he offered generous terms to Lee at Appomattox.

Key 76   Diplomacy and war at sea

OVERVIEW   *The Confederacy sought (and the Union sought to prevent) diplomatic recognition and aid from abroad. The war at sea affected these objectives.*

A naval blockade: Of the South's extensive coast; was declared by Lincoln at the war's outset.
- To pressure Britain and France, the Confederacy attempted an embargo on cotton exports ("King Cotton diplomacy").
- Reserve surpluses and alternate sources (Egypt and India) blunted the strategy.
- England also relied on grain imports from the North.
- The Union Navy secured most of the coast but blockade running continued.
- United States policies on neutral rights on the high seas seemed to contradict its earlier principles. (See Key 35.)

The *Trent* affair: In November 1861 a Union warship removed two Confederate Ambassadors (Mason and Slidell) from a British ship (the *Trent*) off Cuba. Faced with a British ultimatum, Secretary of State Seward had the diplomats released and issued a statement of regret.

Ironclads: In an effort to break the blockade, the Confederacy outfitted an ironclad, the *Virginia* (formerly the *Merrimack*).
- After sinking many wooden vessels, it fought the Union ironclad *Monitor* to a draw (March 9, 1862).
- Smaller gunboats were used effectively by the Union in joint river operations.
- Farragut's fleet took New Orleans (Spring 1862) and Mobile (Summer 1864) using ironclads.
- Securing the Mississippi River divided the Confederate armies.

British aid: "Laird rams" (ironclads) and other vessels were built in Britain for the Confederacy.
- For nearly two years the privateer *Alabama* and other raiders destroyed Union ships on the high seas.
- American interests were ably handled in London by Ambassador Charles Francis Adams.
- American diplomatic pressure finally forced Britain to halt the sale of ships.
- An 1871 treaty arranged by Secretary of State Hamilton Fish settled the Alabama Claims (for damages) with Britain.

The Emancipation Proclamation: Assured that Britain and France would not support a pro-slavery Confederacy despite the impact the Union naval blockade had had on Britain's textile mills and their employees (see Key 79).

Napoleon III: Offered to mediate the war (February 1863) but his offer was spurned by the U.S. as "foreign intervention."
- French armies overthrew the Juarez government of Mexico in June 1863.
- A puppet government was installed under Emperor Maximillian (April 1864).
- U.S. pressure helped cause France to abandon the Mexican adventure after the war (1867).

Key 77 The home front

OVERVIEW *Civilian life, North and South, was significantly altered by the war, but political institutions showed a remarkable continuity.*

Economic impact: The economies of the North and South, after an initial shock, were stimulated by the war.
- War contracts brought prosperity, although workers' wages did not match inflation.
- Speculation, profiteering, and corruption were widespread—some materials were *shoddy* (of poor quality).
- The South became more urbanized, more industrialized, and, despite its states rights doctrine, more centralized politically and economically (see Key 73).
- Northern factory workers became more unionized and more militant, despite employer resistance.

Women: Played a crucial role in the war effort, North and South.
- Many went to work in fields and factories and in government. Society became less patriarchal.
- Dorothea Dix, Superintendent of Nurses, and Clara Barton (later, a founder of the American Red Cross) recruited women for hospital work in the North.
- Dr. Elizabeth Blackwell, first woman medical school graduate, helped persuade the War Department to create the U.S. *Sanitary Commission*, which coordinated volunteer groups.
- Many women teachers with the Freedmen's Aid Commission followed Union troops into *liberated* areas.

The political process: Went on despite the war.
- Congressional elections were held in the North (1862) and South (1863).
- Lincoln's reelection in 1864 was interpreted as a referendum on the war.
- Lincoln effectively mobilized metaphor and Biblical intonation in his wartime speeches. The self-educated president's mastery of language is especially notable in the Gettysburg Address (November 19, 1863), where the concept of national unity was stressed.
- The Second Inaugural (March 4, 1865) declared "Malice toward none; charity for all."

Key 78   Civil rights and Civil War

OVERVIEW *Paradoxically, President Lincoln found it necessary to restrict some civil liberties to gain security and to save the Union and its democratic institutions.*

Wartime government: Congress did not reconvene until July 1861 enabling Lincoln to attempt to suppress the insurrection through the use of presidential war powers.
- Lincoln imposed martial law after a riot in Baltimore, had some Confederate sympathizers jailed, and suspended the writ of habeas corpus.
- Chief Justice Taney, sitting circuit, ruled in *ex parte Merryman* (1861) that Lincoln had acted unconstitutionally, but the president ignored the ruling.
- After the war, in *ex parte Milligan* (1866) the Court struck down the wartime conviction of a civilian by a military tribunal.

Peace Democrats: Opposed continuation of the war. The extreme, "disloyal" faction was branded *Copperheads.*
- Congressman Clement Vallandigham (Ohio), a leading critic, was arrested, exiled to the Confederacy, and then returned by way of Canada.
- Democrats, aided by war weariness, made significant gains in the 1862 Congressional elections.
- Ex-general George McClellan, Democratic presidential candidate in 1864, distanced himself from their peace platform.
- During the war, several thousand dissenters were imprisoned for suspected disloyalty and several hundred newspapers were suppressed for various periods of time.
- Republican Radicals on the Joint Committee on the Conduct of the War pressed for *more* vigorous efforts.

Conscription: Inequities contributed to public unrest.
- It was possible to purchase a substitute or pay for an exemption.
- After the Emancipation Proclamation some poor urban immigrants feared future job competition from blacks.
- Anti-draft riots, with a strong racist tone, in New York City (and elsewhere) were suppressed by federal troops (July 1863).

Key 79 Free at last!

OVERVIEW *Black involvement in the war helped change the Union's objectives, but full emancipation came only with a constitutional amendment.*

Preservation of the Union: Had been Lincoln's avowed objective as the "rebellion" began, but he also saw slavery as a moral evil and a threat to white labor.
- He had considered gradual emancipation and colonization abroad.
- Concern over the border states restrained emancipation early in the war.

Congress: Took the initiative.
- The Confiscation Act of August 1861 encouraged slaves ("contraband") to escape.
- In April 1862 Congress abolished slavery in the District of Columbia and, in June, in the Western territories.

The Emancipation Proclamation (effective January 1, 1863): Based on "military necessity."
- It freed slaves in areas in rebellion but not in areas controlled by the Union. Therefore, not one slave was immediately freed.
- The war's purpose now took on a moral tone.
- British and French diplomatic recognition of the Confederacy was now unlikely.

Blacks: Not accepted into the military initially, they became important in the Union war effort.
- After Congress authorized recruitment (1862), over 185,000 blacks served in the navy and army (85% of those eligible; 10% of the Union Army). They won 23 Congressional Medals of Honor.
- Blacks desired combat but were often given menial tasks (and were paid less until 1864). All their officers were white.
- Colonel Robert Gould Shaw's **54th Massachusetts** (black) **Regiment** stormed Ft. Wagner (South Carolina), suffering 40% casualties. Other black units served with distinction.
- There were incidents of anti-black racial violence and discrimination in the North.

Emancipation: Was finally secured by passage of the 13th Amendment.
- At Lincoln's urging, the proposal was included in the 1864 Republican Platform.
- The ratification process was completed in December 1865.

Key 80   A "New Revolution"

OVERVIEW *The American Civil War brought revolutionary changes in warfare, but more important, produced significant economic and political changes in the country.*

The first modern war: Produced a revolution in military technology
and strengthened *defense.*
- Firepower was greatly enhanced (in range, accuracy, and rate of
  fire).
- Breech-loading rifles, repeating carbines, and the *Burton bullet*
  were patented.
- The Ordinance Bureau helped transform American industry.
  Arsenals applied machinery to processes (*the American System*),
  which were widely copied abroad.
- The war accelerated the use of new *civilian* technology:
  1. McCormick's reaper helped provide needed grain.
  2. Singer's sewing machine facilitated the production of uniforms.
  3. Machines turned out inexpensive shoes, for both the military
     and civilians. Standardized sizes were adopted.
  4. Mass markets for manufactured goods at reduced prices
     developed.

Economic legislation: Blocked by the South before the war, was now
passed by Congress (most of it in 1862).
- An *excise tax* and the first graduated *income tax* were enacted to
  help finance the war.
- Congress authorized a limited issue of new paper *currency*
  (greenbacks).
- The national *Banking Acts* stimulated sale of government bonds.
- Higher protective *tariffs* were enacted (average rates were doubled).
- The *Homestead Act* provided 160 acres of free land to settlers
  who resided on it for five years.
- Chartering and funding began for a *transcontinental railroad.*
- The Morrill Land Grant Act encouraged the establishment of
  state universities.
- The 1864 *Contract Labor Act* assisted the importing of immi-
  grant labor.

Republican Party: The coalition of free labor, western agriculture, and
eastern business was strengthened by the above legislation.

Government and business: Became closely allied. The government
vastly increased its direct impact on individual citizens.

Theme 13 RECONSTRUCTION

*P*olicies for dealing with a defeated Confederacy and with freed former slaves were reluctantly formulated as the war progressed. The executive and legislative branches came into conflict over reconstruction plans, climaxing in the impeachment of Lincoln's successor. Radical Republican governments in the South achieved some limited successes but were hampered by growing white Southern resistance. A general decline in political morality and honesty occurred during the eight years of the Grant Administration. After a compromise settled the disputed 1876 election, military reconstruction was terminated. Racism was still very evident, but Reconstruction amendments and laws were to provide the bases for a "Second Reconstruction" a century later (the civil rights movement of the 1950s and 1960s).

INDIVIDUAL KEYS IN THIS THEME

Key 81   The devastated South

OVERVIEW   *The Civil War left the economies of the eleven seceded states in shambles and the pre-war social system in disarray.*

Physical destruction: Widespread in the South, where most of the fighting had taken place.
- Sherman's March to the Sea had left desolation in its wake: a preview of Modern War.
- In some cases Confederates employed *scorched earth* tactics.
- Major cities (Richmond, Petersburg, Charleston) had been besieged.
- Guerrilla warfare had devastated border states.

The South's economy: Largely in ruins:
- Crops, livestock, and structures of both planters and small farmers were heavily damaged or destroyed.
- The area's inadequate industrial structure was largely inoperative.
- Confederate money and bonds were worthless.
- The market for cash crops (cotton, sugar, tobacco) had shriveled.
- Emancipation had freed the South's slave labor supply.
- Capital was in very short supply.

Society: The pre-war **social hierarchy** was shaken.
- Over 250,000 Confederate soldiers lay dead.
- Both white and black refugees roamed the land, though most continued to work.
- Plantation aristocrats experienced a temporary loss of power.
- Fears of insurrection by former slaves were revived.

Confederate governments: National, state, and local, were deposed.
- Jefferson Davis and a few others served brief prison terms.
- Many former Confederate politicians quickly returned to public life (see Key 84).
- There were no treason or "war crimes" trials except that of Henry Wirz, who had commanded the Andersonville, Georgia prisoner of war camp. (The Union had had its counterparts at Elmira, New York and elsewhere.)

Key 82   Rehearsals for Reconstruction

OVERVIEW *Policies for dealing with liberated Confederate territory were necessary early in the war, but a comprehensive plan emerged only slowly.*

Border states and occupied areas: Provided the first opportunities for federal *reconstruction* of the South.
- Mountainous Western counties of Virginia, with few slaves, rejected secession in 1861 and were admitted as a separate state (West Virginia, 1863).
- Lincoln appointed military governors in areas of Louisiana, Arkansas, and western Tennessee occupied by Union troops.
- Some Union officers used runaway slaves as "contraband of war."
- When General John C. Fremont proclaimed the emancipation of slaves held by rebel masters in Missouri, Lincoln had the order retracted.

The Sea Islands experiment: Began when the Navy occupied offshore South Carolina islands in late 1861.
- After the planters fled, idealistic Northern reformers promoted a model black free-labor economy.
- Speculators bought land at auction, and many blacks returned to paid labor on cotton farms.

The Confiscation Act of 1862: Gave the president authority to use seized rebel property for the Union war effort, including slaves held by Confederate soldiers. The act also provided for amnesty (pardon) under certain conditions.

Occupied New Orleans: General Benjamin Butler administered a loyalty oath and held elections that sent two representatives to Congress. Louisiana's 1864 constitution abolished slavery, but Lincoln's suggestion for limited black suffrage was resisted.

The Freedmen's Bureau: Was set up by Congress in March 1865 to provide for the immediate needs of refugees and freedmen.
- Confiscated and abandoned lands could be rented and sold to freedmen. False rumors persisted that "40 acres and a mule" would be distributed as outright gifts.
- Under General O. O. Howard, labor contract agreements were formulated.
- The Bureau established schools and hospitals and provided courts to settle legal disputes involving freed blacks.

Key 83   Lincoln and Congress plans

OVERVIEW   *The executive and legislative branches differed in their views of how the seceded states should constitutionally be restored to the Union.*

Conflict: President Lincoln and the **Congress** differed on the status of the seceded states.
- The Constitution mentions neither a right of secession nor provisions for readmission of states.
- To Lincoln the eleven rebellious states had never legally left the Union, making rapid restoration possible under presidential administration.
- Radicals argued that Congress should administer the seceded states as conquered territories.
- In *Texas v. White* (1869) the Supreme Court described the Union as constitutionally "indestructible."

Lincoln's 10% Plan: A Proclamation of Amnesty and Reconstruction (December 8, 1863) was issued under his presidential pardoning power.
- When 10% of those who had voted in 1860 took an oath of loyalty a state government could be organized.
- Top Confederate officials would be excluded from pardon, but some well-qualified blacks would be allowed to vote.

Loyal state governments: Were organized in Louisiana and Arkansas (Spring 1864) and in Tennessee (February 1865). However, Congress refused to recognize their electoral votes or seat their representatives after the 1864 election.

Congressional Reconstruction: Proposed in the Wade-Davis Bill (July 1864).
- A *majority* of white male citizens would have to swear they had never been disloyal.
- A state constitutional convention would be required to abolish slavery and repudiate secession.
- The bill was pocket vetoed by Lincoln.

The Wade-Davis Manifesto (August 1864): Declared the authority of Congress to be paramount and advised the president to "confine himself to his executive duties and leave political reorganization to Congress." Congress and the president were stalemated at the time of Appomattox and the Lincoln assassination.

Key 84   Johnson and Congress

OVERVIEW *Clashing views on Reconstruction between the president and a radical Congress led to a constitutional and political crisis.*

Andrew Johnson: Became president after Lincoln's assassination.
- Born in poverty, becoming literate as an adult, Johnson hated Southern planter aristocrats.
- A War Democrat, he remained in the Senate when his state (Tennessee) seceded.
- He was appointed military governor when Union armies occupied most of the state.
- In 1864 he was elected vice president with Lincoln on the Union ticket.
- Radicals at first believed he was their ally.

Johnson's plan: Similar to Lincoln's, it provided for rapid restoration of the Southern states.
- With Congress in recess Johnson issued two proclamations in May 1865:
  1. A new Amnesty Proclamation with a longer list of exclusions, particularly large property holders (Johnson then issued numerous individual pardons).
  2. Provision for steps to return states to the Union eliminated Lincoln's 10% provision but required ratification of the Thirteenth Amendment and repudiation of secession and of Confederate debts.
- In December Congress reconvened and denied seats to Southern representatives (including former Confederate leaders).
- Without distribution of land, without political or educational guarantees, Southern blacks were now burdened with restrictive *Black Codes*.

Radical Republicans: Angered by Southern resistance, they become more militant.
- A Joint Committee on Reconstruction was dominated by **Thaddeus Stevens** (Pennsylvania), **Charles Sumner** (Massachusetts), and **Ben Wade** (Ohio).
- Humanitarian concerns (to assure the rights of freed former slaves) were mixed with partisan political motives (to delay the return of Democrats and to cement Republican Party control).
- In 1866 Johnson vetoed renewal of the Freedmen's Bureau.

- The next month a civil rights bill was passed over his veto.

Fourteenth Amendment: Was approved by Congress in June 1866.
- Freedmen citizens' privileges and immunities were protected.
- "Due process of law" and "equal protection of the law" were guaranteed (but not to women explicitly).
- Johnson spoke against the amendment, and ten Southern states rejected it.
- Although the Courts later used the amendment to protect corporations, it became the basis for most modern civil rights cases.
- The Amendment was later used to apply most of the Bill of Rights to the states.

1866 Congressional election: Johnson's "swing around the circle" appeal to the public failed. The Radicals gained over a two-thirds majority in Congress.

Congressional Reconstruction Acts (March 1867): Passed over Johnson vetoes.
- Military Reconstruction Act: a moderate compromise, required acceptance of the Fourteenth Amendment and black suffrage by the South.
  1. Ten states were divided into five military districts.
  2. Statehood could result from a constitution approved by adult males (white and black).
- Command of the Army Act: limited the president's military authority.
- Tenure of Office Act: required Senate approval for *removal* of presidential appointees.
- The Supreme Court's power to review Reconstruction policy was also restricted by Congressional action.

Impeachment of Johnson: Based on his violation of the Tenure of Office Act when he tried to remove Secretary of War Stanton. This was clearly a political move on the part of the Radicals.
- The House of Representatives voted impeachment charges (February 1868).
- After a three-month trial in the Senate (Johnson was not present), the vote for conviction (and removal from office) fell one vote short of the necessary two-thirds.
- Johnson served out his last few months, with Radical Reconstruction in control.

Key 85   Grant

OVERVIEW *The two terms of General U. S. Grant spanned most of the Reconstruction period and were marked by an extraordinary amount of corruption.*

Election of 1868:
- Republican Convention endorsed Radical Reconstruction and nominated war hero Ulysses S. Grant for president.
- The Democrats nominated the wartime governor of New York, Horatio Seymour.
- The Republicans "waved the bloody shirt" and won a close popular majority due to the black vote.

Fifteenth Amendment: Enfranchising black voters, it was adopted in 1870 only after Southern states were required to ratify it.

Election of 1872: Horace Greeley, editor of the New York *Tribune,* was the presidential candidate of both the Liberal Republicans (who had bolted the party over the issue of political corruption) and the Democrats. Grant won reelection easily.

Political corruption: In an era of materialism and greed.
- The Democratic **Tweed Ring** in New York City and the Republican **Gas Ring** in Philadelphia were examples of municipal political theft.
- **Jim Fiske** and **Jay Gould** plotted with Grant's brother-in-law to corner the gold market, leading to a Black Friday crash (September 24, 1869).
- In the **Credit Mobilier** scandal, profits from construction of the Union Pacific Railroad went to the road's promoters.
- Other examples were the "whiskey ring" fraud and the bribing of the Secretary of War by corrupt Indian agents.
- A "salary grab" act increasing congressional and presidential pay retroactively aroused public anger.
- Scandals and depression led to Democratic gains in the 1874 Congressional elections.

Economic problems:
- Although the Grant administration favored "sound money," greenbacks were only partially removed from circulation.
- The Panic of 1873 began a six-year depression.
- The Redemption Act of 1875 provided payment for greenbacks in gold.

Key 86　Radical Reconstruction and white resistance

OVERVIEW　*A decade of Radical Republican Reconstruction in the South fell short of its promise and potential.*

Southern states: New state constitutions were written by conventions (under military supervision). After ratifying the Fourteenth Amendment all but three former Confederate states were admitted in 1868.
- Universal manhood suffrage, legislative reapportionment, and civil rights protections for blacks were included.
- Public (segregated) schools and social services were established.
- Criminal codes were reformed; rights of women extended.
- Economic recovery programs were initiated.
- No provision was made for land confiscation or distribution, however.

A Republican coalition: Secured political power in the South.
- *Carpetbaggers* were Northerners who moved South after the war. Some were veterans seeking economic opportunity. Others were idealistic teachers or missionaries.
- *Scalawags* (Southern white Republicans often in mountainous, Union areas) were also reviled by Conservative Democrats.
- Union Leagues and the Freedmen's Bureau also supported the coalition.
- Blacks never held political office equal to their proportion in the population.
  1. Two black U.S. Senators (from Mississippi) and 14 black members of the House of Representatives were elected, but no governors.
  2. Some served in all Southern state legislatures.
  3. Despite inexperience and limited education, many blacks made significant political contributions.
- Republican governments were criticized for "lavish" spending (higher taxes and debt) and political corruption, but this was a *national* phenomenon of the time (see Key 85).

White resistance: Was accompanied by a reemergence of racism (North and South).
- The **Ku Klux Klan** (organized in Tennessee in late 1865) intimi-

dated and terrorized blacks and white Republicans through the South.
- Other groups (Knights of the White Camellia, South Carolina Red Shirts) also resorted to whippings and murder.
- The white social hierarchy was gradually restored to power.

Three Enforcement Acts: Passed by Congress in 1870–71, sought to protect freedmen's right to vote, supervise elections, and outlaw Klan activities. By late 1871 the KKK had been crushed by vigorous federal action.

Civil Rights Act of 1875: Sought to assure equal accommodations in public places and black participation on juries.
- No means of enforcement were provided.
- Key portions were declared unconstitutional by the Supreme Court in 1883, when it ruled that discrimination by private individuals was not illegal.

Radical Reconstruction: Continued to fade.
- All but three Southern Republican governments were "redeemed" by Conservative Democrats by 1876.
- The North tired of the "Southern problem" and Republican Stalwarts turned their attention to other concerns.
- The most vigorous Radical leaders, such as Thaddeus Stevens and Charles Sumner, had died.
- For generations the "Solid South" would be dominated by the Democratic Party.

Key 87   Compromise of 1877: End of Reconstruction

OVERVIEW *The compromise settling the disputed election of 1876 brought an effective end to Reconstruction.*

Election of 1876:
- Though backed by Stalwart Republicans, Grant withdrew from seeking a third presidential term.
- Frontrunner James G. Blaine was denied the Republican nomination after the "Mulligan letters" revealed alleged railroad company bribes.
- Governor **Rutherford B. Hayes** of Ohio became the Republican candidate.
- His Democratic opponent was **Samuel J. Tilden**, reform governor of New York, who had helped to smash the Tweed Ring.
- The Republicans were hurt by the depression and by Grant administration scandals and Reconstruction policies.
- Republicans gained by "waving the bloody shirt" (reviving wartime bitterness).

Disputed results:
- Tilden, with a popular majority, was one electoral vote short, with 19 votes from three Southern states in dispute.
- A special electoral commission voted 8 to 7 along party lines for Hayes, who would win by 185 to 184.
- With control of two houses of Congress split, a constitutional crisis loomed.
- In the so-called Compromise of 1877, a bargain was struck:
  1. The last federal troops would leave South Carolina and Louisiana.
  2. Republicans would pledge financial aid and patronage to Southern states.
  3. The election of Hayes would be certified.

Redemption (return to home rule):
- Occupation by federal troops ended in the South.
- Conservative Democratic control returned (the *Solid South*).
- Hayes appointed an ex-Confederate as Postmaster-General.
- Reconciliation came at the expense of blacks: *Jim Crow* segregation laws began to be passed through the South.
- Thousands of disillusioned Southern blacks migrated to Kansas (*Exodusters*) in 1877.

GLOSSARY

abolition   A moral crusade to immediately end the system of human slavery in the United States.

Africanisms   Features from African cultures that survived the transporting of black slaves to the Americas.

American System   Congressman Henry Clay's plan in the 1820s for a protective tariff and federal financing of "internal improvements" (transportation systems). Also, the factory system featuring interchangeable parts and mass production.

Anti-Federalists   Those who opposed the adoption of the Constitution of 1787 and its grant of additional powers to the central government.

Bill of Rights   The first ten amendments to the Constitution, that protect individual rights from the power of government.

black codes   Restrictive laws, particularly in the South, designed to regulate and control slaves and free African-Americans before the Civil War (slave codes) or former slaves after the war. *Example:* Vagrancy laws.

blockade   An effort to close the ports and coast of the enemy to foreign trade (as the Union navy attempted with the Confederacy).

bloody shirt,   The attempt to gain post-Civil War political
waving the   advantage by emphasizing supposed party connections with loyalty (Radical Republicans) or rebellion (Democrats).

border states   Those peripheral states in which some slaves were held but which did not join the Confederacy.

boycott

An agreement to not purchase or use certain goods in an effort to influence the economic and political policies of the producer.

carpetbaggers

Derogatory term applied to Northerners who went South after the Civil War, often for economic or political opportunity but also frequently for idealistic reasons.

civil disobedience

Intentionally breaking or defying law to call attention to what is believed to be evil or injustice.

compact theory

The idea (advanced by Rousseau, Locke, and Jefferson) that government is created by voluntary agreement among the people involved and that revolution is justified if government breaks the compact by exceeding its authority.

confederation

A political system in which the central government is relatively weak and member states retain considerable sovereignty.

Copperheads

Derogatory term applied to "disloyal" or antiwar figures (often Democrats) inside the Union during the Civil War.

cultural diffusion

Imitativeness; the adoption of cultural features of one people by another (example: mutual cultural adoptions by Europeans, Native Americans, and African Americans).

draft

A conscription system for compulsory armed service used by both sides during the Civil War.

draft riots

Mob violence opposing conscription laws during the Civil War; the most violent occurred in New York City (July 1863).

emancipation

Setting free, as in various plans for ending slavery, finally completely accomplished by the Thirteenth Amendment.

embargo	An attempt to withhold goods from export in order to influence the policies of the former purchasers.
Enlightenment	A European intellectual movement that stressed the use of human reason.
factions	Political groups that agree on objectives and policies; the origins of political parties.
federal system	A political structure that divides power between the national government and its member states.
Federalist Papers	Essays written by Madison, Hamilton, and Jay in support of ratification of the new (second) United States Constitution.
feudalism	Medieval economic and political traditions, few of which survived in the New World and were dealt a death blow by the American Revolution.
filibuster	Private military adventures seeking to establish American control abroad, particularly in the Caribbean area. Also prolonged congressional debate used as a legislative delaying tactic.
Free soil	Movement that opposed the expansion of slavery through banning its importation into western territories.
Freedmen's Bureau	Agency created by Congress as the war ended to assist Civil War refugees and freed former slaves.
frontier	The area (usually in the West) where European settlements touched "unoccupied" territory. Also the borders between nations.
fugitive slave laws	Legislation designed to capture and return slaves who had escaped from their owners.

gag rule	An attempt to block discussion of anti-slavery petitions in the House of Representatives, 1836–44.
Glorious Revolution	The English "Bloodless Revolution" of 1688–89 that replaced the Stuart monarchy with Protestants William and Mary.
gold rush	The "49ers" flocked to California after the discovery of gold in that territory (statehood soon followed).
Great Awakening	Several waves of evangelical religious revivalism which swept through America.
Great Migration	The mass movement of Puritans from England to the Western Hemisphere in the 17th century.
head right	A grant of land, usually 500 acres, used as an incentive to attract settlers to a colony.
Homestead Act	Legislation designed to encourage settlement by having the government offer free or inexpensive land.
immigration	The voluntary movement of people permanently from their homelands to a new area.
impeachment	The Constitutional power granted to the legislature to bring public officials to trial and, if convicted, to remove them from office.
impressment	The forced recruitment or reclaiming of sailors who had deserted. One cause cited for the second United States war with Britain.
indentured servitude	A contract to provide labor for a specified time to pay off passage money to the New World.
Industrial Revolution	The conversion to machinery and to new sources of energy (primarily steam power).

ironclads	Wooden ships with metal armor that were employed by both sides during the Civil War.
isolationism	A policy that avoids involvement in foreign alliances and wars.
joint stock companies	Chartered to empower the raising of capital (money) through the sale of shares representing partial ownership of a company.
judicial review	The power of the courts to pass on the constitutionality of acts of the legislature and actions of the executive branch.
Ku Klux Klan	Organized to intimidate and terrorize freed blacks and "carpetbaggers" and to restore white supremacy in the post-Civil War South.
labor unions	Workers' organizations formed for the purpose of seeking improvements in wages and working conditions.
Loyalists	Those "Tories" (some estimate as high as one-third) who remained loyal to England during the American Revolution.
Manifest Destiny	The conviction that the United States would inevitably expand its territory to its "continental limits" or beyond.
martial law	Military authority supplanting civil law and administration in a war zone.
mercantilism	An economic system in which a nation regulates commerce to gain wealth through a favorable trade balance with its colonies.
Monroe Doctrine	A United States policy that sought to insulate the Western Hemisphere from European intervention.
nationalism	An attitude that gives highest allegiance to the nation-state rather than localities, member states, or the international community.

Native Americans   The earliest human inhabitants of the Western Hemisphere, mistakenly named "Indians" by early European explorers.

nativism   An attitude or policy that favors native inhabitants over immigrants, or later arrivals.

natural rights   Those rights that the Enlightenment (and Jefferson's "Declaration") saw as inherent for all humans and that government is not justified in violating.

neutrality   A policy that avoids favoring either belligerent (impartiality) in a war in which your nation is not involved.

Northwest Passage   A water route through North America (ice-bound much of the year) to reach Asia from Europe.

nullification   The doctrine that a state may overrule federal government actions or legislation with which it disagrees.

panics   Cycles of economic depressions, often beginning with bank failures.

patents   A government conferring of exclusive right to make and sell an invention.

patroons   Dutch settlers (proprietors) who received large Hudson Valley estates or tracts of land as an incentive to populate the area.

plantations   Large farms or estates raising staple cash crops and, in the South, often employing slave labor. Also the general system of "planting" new American colonies.

popular sovereignty   The policy that the status of slavery should be decided by popular vote within a territory (also sometimes called "squatter sovereignty").

prohibition The movement to legally forbid the manufacture and sale of alcoholic beverages.

Puritans Dissenters who sought to "purify" the Church of England from within and who initially populated much of New England.

Reconstruction Programs for restoration of former Confederate states to the Union following the Civil War.

Romanticism An intellectual movement that stressed emotion, sentiment, and individualism. A reaction to rationalism and the classical revival.

scalawags A derisive term applied to Southern whites who cooperated with post-Civil War Republican Reconstruction.

secession The right of a member state to withdraw from the Union if action of the federal government infringed on its rights.

sectionalism Giving priority to the concerns of one's region rather than to those of the nation as a whole.

specie "Hard" currency (gold or silver) as opposed to more inflationary paper money.

spoils system The winning political party inherits the right to appoint its loyal supporters to positions in government.

squatters Frontier migrants who settled on lands without clear legal claim to it.

states rights According to the compact theory of the Union the states retained all powers not specifically delegated to the central government by the Constitution.

strict construction The principle that the national government is legally granted only those powers specifically delegated in the Constitution (opposite: "loose" construction).

suffrage   The ballot, or right to vote. Widened for white males in the era of Jackson.

tariff   A tax on imports (also referred to as a "duty"); taxes on *exports* are banned by the Constitution. A "protective" tariff has rates high enough to discourage imports.

36°30' Line   The Missouri Compromise provided that slavery would be banned in territories north of this parallel but territories south of the line would be open to slavery.

transcendentalism A New England cultural and social movement based on the idea of human nature being able to "transcend" or go beyond rational experience.

underground   A system or network for assisting runaway
railroad   slaves to reach freedom in Northern states or a foreign country.

utopian   Attempts to establish ideal cooperative societies
communities   based on religious, economic, or philosophical principles.

War Hawks   Those members of Congress who favored a second war with Britain in 1812, in most cases seeking territorial expansion.

Whig Party   A national political coalition formed to oppose the Jacksonian Democrats.

witchcraft   A belief that humans may be able to exercise supernatural powers for evil purposes. Persecution of persons accused of witchcraft spread from Europe to the American colonies in the late 17th century.

writs of assistance General search warrants employed by Britain in an effort to prevent smuggling in the American colonies.

INDEX